TABLE OF CONTENTS

Copyright © Mometrix Media. You have been licensed one copy of this document for personal use only.
Any other reproduction or redistribution is strictly prohibited. All rights reserved.

Top 20 Test Taking Tips

1. Carefully follow all the test registration procedures
2. Know the test directions, duration, topics, question types, how many questions
3. Setup a flexible study schedule at least 3-4 weeks before test day
4. Study during the time of day you are most alert, relaxed, and stress free
5. Maximize your learning style; visual learner use visual study aids, auditory learner use auditory study aids
6. Focus on your weakest knowledge base
7. Find a study partner to review with and help clarify questions
8. Practice, practice, practice
9. Get a good night's sleep; don't try to cram the night before the test
10. Eat a well balanced meal
11. Know the exact physical location of the testing site; drive the route to the site prior to test day
12. Bring a set of ear plugs; the testing center could be noisy
13. Wear comfortable, loose fitting, layered clothing to the testing center; prepare for it to be either cold or hot during the test
14. Bring at least 2 current forms of ID to the testing center
15. Arrive to the test early; be prepared to wait and be patient
16. Eliminate the obviously wrong answer choices, then guess the first remaining choice
17. Pace yourself; don't rush, but keep working and move on if you get stuck
18. Maintain a positive attitude even if the test is going poorly
19. Keep your first answer unless you are positive it is wrong
20. Check your work, don't make a careless mistake

Copyright © Mometrix Media. You have been licensed one copy of this document for personal use only. Any other reproduction or redistribution is strictly prohibited. All rights reserved.

Why Certify?

PMP: Project Management Professional
- Raise the standards in your field and distinguish your experience.
- Use your credentials to further your career.
- Improve your skills and abilities to manage workers

Official Website:
http://www.pmi.org
http://www.pmi.org

Score

The Project Management Professional (PMP) Certification Examination measures the application of knowledge, skills, tools, and techniques that are utilized in the practice of project management. The examination specifications were established in 1997 after the Project Management Institute completed a job analysis study. The PMP Certification Examination is comprised of 200 four-option multiple-choice questions that are developed and validated by PMPs. The examination is reviewed and revised annually to satisfy the examination test specifications and to ensure that each question has a referenced source.

Cost of Exam:

Project Management Professional (PMP®)		
Initial Certification Fee – member of PMI in good standing	$405	€ 340
Initial Certification Fee – non member of PMI	$555	€ 465
Re-Examination Fee – member of PMI in good standing	$275	€ 230
Re-Examination Fee – non member of PMI	$375	€ 315

Copyright © Mometrix Media. You have been licensed one copy of this document for personal use only. Any other reproduction or redistribution is strictly prohibited. All rights reserved.

Project Management Professional

Project management and operations management

Organization management refers to managing the production of the same product or service on an ongoing, repetitive basis, such as the manufacture of cars. Project management refers to the oversight and planning of a temporary product or service, such a developing a tracking system for car sales throughout the country. Once the system has been developed, that project has ended, but the organization is still producing and selling cars.

Strategic plan, portfolio management, program management, and project management

Strategic plans, which define the parameters of a project, are often developed and revised around the following factors:
- Customer or market demand
- Customer request
- Advances in technology or other pertinent areas
- Changes in the law or government standards
- Political climate
- Etc.

Strategic Plans refer to the overall priorities and long-term goals of an organization. Portfolio Management refers to the management of a group of programs or projects that serve to meet, or fall within the parameters, of the overall strategic plan. It may include several portfolios, which contain programs and projects. Program Management is the coordination of various programs and projects that together achieve and support the strategic plan. Project Management monitors and controls the production of products, services or results that are part of a program, which may be part of a portfolio, all of which fit within the parameters of the overall strategic plan. All organizations may or may not have portfolios and programs, but they will all have long-term strategic plans, and projects that fulfill those plans.

Project and ongoing work effort

A project can be defined by the following elements:
- Temporary – not necessarily short term
- Creates a unique product, service or result
- Reaches its end when the objectives are completed, or when it is determined that the objectives cannot be met.
- Results of a project can be a product, a change in procedures or staffing, change in an organization's overall structure, or a new system such as an information system.

Copyright © Mometrix Media. You have been licensed one copy of this document for personal use only. Any other reproduction or redistribution is strictly prohibited. All rights reserved.

An ongoing work effort is a repetitive process that is part of an organization's regular processes or procedures. Projects often include ongoing work efforts in addition to focused, temporary work procedures.

Key factors in projects

Key factors of a project are:
- Budget
- Schedule
- Scope
- Quality
- Stakeholders

The scope of a project is how extensive or inclusive it is, such as changing one procedure, or redesigning all of the procedures of an organization. Stakeholders are those people involved in the project or in the organization that have a particular interest or goal that is affected by the project, such as company administrators. The scope and quality of a project can be impacted by the goals of the stakeholders, the budget and other resources, and the schedule. In other words, if a result is needed in a shorter amount of time, or the budget is reduced, the scope or quality of the project may be compromised. A good project manager will balance all of these factors as effectively as possible.

Project phases

Every project experiences four basic phases, called the project cycle:
- Initiation of the project

- Planning and organizing the project
- Implementing or installing the product or service
- Closing the project

There are three basic ways in which phases relate to each other:
- Sequential – one phase follows another. This allows for project management to reassess the project, and the balance between scope and resources, between phases.
- Overlapping – one phase starts while the previous phase is in place, such implementing while the project is still in the planning phase. Although this may hurry the project along, it also poses the risk of not allowing proper assessment during the project.
- Iterative – one phase completely ends, and then project management begins the next phase. This is more time consuming, but may be applicable to a project that is tentative in nature.

Project cycles and product cycles

Project cycles refer to the phases of a project, and end with the completion of the project. Product cycles refer to the life of the product, and go on indefinitely, or until the product is replaced or no longer produced. An example is a tracking system for a car manufacturer. Once the tracking system is in place, the project cycle has completed its closing

Copyright © Mometrix Media. You have been licensed one copy of this document for personal use only. Any other reproduction or redistribution is strictly prohibited. All rights reserved.

stage, and the temporary project is complete. However, the tracking system, which is the product, will continue to be operative until it is replaced, ended, or perhaps indefinitely. The structure of a project cycle in relation to resources and other factors, tends to be that the level of risk and uncertainty diminishes from initiation to closing, while the cost and other resource uses tends to increase throughout the cycle of the project. If the benefit outweighs the cost, the level of risk and uncertainty drops.

Project initiation and organizational structures and cultures

The type of organizational structure can also impact and define a project. Structure types can range from functional, meaning each employee reports to one superior, and is responsible for one area, to projectized, which refers to an organization that is flexible around the needs of a project. The culture of an organization refers to the values and relationships of the people affecting decisions. When initiating a project, one should take into account the resources including staff, his/her role in the organization, etc. In other words, if the organization is functional so that each employee is tied to a particular task, but the managers have a culture of wanting to see progress in the company, a project manager can work with a other managers to somewhat suspend or alter the functional organization in order to get a project accomplished.

Stakeholders

Some of the key types of stakeholders include but are not limited to:

- Customers or end users – those who will use, buy, or participate in the end use of a product
- Sponsor – a person who provides support for the project, either financially or politically within an organization
- Portfolio managers – people responsible for a group of projects or programs, and who assess a project in terms of the larger portfolio
- Program managers – people responsible for particular programs, such as computer maintenance, into which the project fits
- Project managers – responsible for the end result of the project, and for incorporating the needs of other stakeholders
- Functional managers – responsible for key functional areas, such as human resources
- Operations managers – responsible for operations such as manufacturing
- Sellers or business partners – suppliers who provide parts of/for a project

Every project is affected and somewhat defined by its stakeholders, those people who have an interest, or a stake in the outcome. Stakeholders can be internal, such as project or organizational managers, or external, such as financial sponsors or end users or customers. It is pivotal to the end success, and cost-

- 8 -

Copyright © Mometrix Media. You have been licensed one copy of this document for personal use only. Any other reproduction or redistribution is strictly prohibited. All rights reserved.

effectiveness, of the project that all stakeholders are identified and incorporated into the project. For example, if organizational management wants a product changed, which is a type of project, but the end customer will have to pay a higher price for the new product and therefore possibly not buy the product, the project manager needs to incorporate and balance the needs of these and other stakeholders before initiating the project, to avoid possible problems later that would result in the success or failure of the project.

Organizational process assets

Organizational process assets are those process, procedures, or collections of data that serve as both resources and parameters for project planning. Processes and procedures include but are not limited to:

- Standard procedures and policies
- Project planning and work breakdown templates
- Communication procedures and guidelines
- Project closure guidelines
- Financial forms and requirements
- Change and risk control procedures

Collections of data include but are not limited to:

- Historical information
- Process measurement databases
- Financial databases
- Project files

A project may be impacted by, and may also affect, existing organizational process assets.

Managing and balancing processes

Effective project management involves first selecting those processes that are needed to accomplish the project objectives, and then managing the knowledge, skills, tools and activities needed to complete the project. Project management may involve tailoring the processes of an organization to fit the requirements of the project. Effective project management also means balancing the scope, time, quality, and resources with the processes and requirements within the organization. Project management usually falls into two main categories:

- Project processes – the smooth flow of the project through its existence using the appropriate processes
- Product-oriented processes – processes that are defined by the project life cycle

Project processes

Any project undertaken within an organization must be planned and implemented within the processes and parameters of the organization, which means it is not a closed system. Project management includes carefully addressing each process and its inputs, its tools and techniques, as well as the resulting output, or result, of the project. Projects in turn deliver products,

Copyright © Mometrix Media. You have been licensed one copy of this document for personal use only. Any other reproduction or redistribution is strictly prohibited. All rights reserved.

information, capabilities, etc., back to the organization. Effective project management involves integrating and coordinating the goals and processes of the project with the processes of the organization. Project management processes generally fall into five categories:

- Initiating – processes to define a new project, or to get authorization for the project
- Planning – processes that define the scope and objective(s) of the project
- Monitoring – processes that track and regulate the performance of the project
- Executing – processes performed to complete the project
- Closing – processes to finalize all activities across all process groups

Project phases are sequential parts of a project life cycle such as initiation, execution, and close. Project processes are actions and activities that are performed as needed throughout the project life cycle. Process groups may apply to the whole project, or to a phase of a project. The five process groups are generally sequential, in that each group is usually followed by the next group, but they also interact with and affect each other. For instance, if one phase of a project included a test run of a product, the test run itself would undergo the five process groups, from initiating to closing. However, through the five process groups, the scope of the test run – which would have been established during the

Initiation Process Group – might change because during the Monitoring Process Group it was discovered that the test run was not long enough to thoroughly test the product that will be the final result of the project.

Initiating process group

The Initiating Process Group develops, defines, and identifies the project, or phase of a project. It includes obtaining authorization for the project or phase. The Initiation Process Group is usually performed at the beginning of each phase, to confirm that the project is still valid, still represents the stakeholders, and whether it should be continued. It also confirms the success criteria, or the measurements to determine if the project or phase is successful. This process group contains two main subgroups:

- Develop Project Charter – this step officially defines, validates and authorizes a project.
- Project Stakeholders – as part of a process group, this step re-identifies stakeholders and their needs.

Each of the five process groups includes interrelated inputs and outputs. Generally for the Initiating Process Group, the input/output cycle is: describing the work (input) develops a charter (output) which then becomes the input for redefining the stakeholders (output).

Planning process group

Copyright © Mometrix Media. You have been licensed one copy of this document for personal use only. Any other reproduction or redistribution is strictly prohibited. All rights reserved.

The Planning Process Group is the most comprehensive of the process groups. It develops specific actions to perform the scope of the project or phase that is identified by the Initiating Process Group. This process group may be required because it is discovered that the project or phase needs to be refined, and the course(s) of action need(s) to be changed. This is sometimes referred to as rolling wave planning. Some of the subgroups of this process group are:

- Develop Project Management Plan – preparing and coordinating the actions needed to implement the project charter.
- Collect Requirements – defining and documenting stakeholder needs.Scope – a detailed description of the project or phase.
- Create Work Breakdown Structure (WBS) – dividing the project or phase into manageable components.And Sequence Activities – identify activities and the relationship between the activities.
- Develop Schedule – analyze activity sequences and schedule restraints to produce a schedule.

Subgroups of the Planning Process Group not related to defining and developing are:

- Estimate Activity Resources and Durations – estimate type and quantities of material, equipment and supplies, also the number of work periods needed.

- Estimate Costs and Determine Budget – develop approximation of resources needed; coordinate all the cost information to develop an overall budget for project or phase.
- Plan Quality – develop rubric and/or criteria for how success of the project or phase can be measured.
- Develop Human Resource Plan – identify participating personnel, roles and responsibilities.
- Plan Communications – determine stakeholder information needs and develop a communication plan.
- Plan Risk Management – develop how risk management will be conducted.Risks. Perform Qualitative and Quantitative Risk Analysis – identify the type and number of possible risks to the project/phase and prioritize according to potential effect.
- Plan Risk Responses – develop options and actions in response to risks.
- Plan Procurements – document purchasing decisions and identify vendors.

Executing process group

The Executing Process Group implements and integrates the activities defined in the Planning Process Group, and coordinates people and resources. It is the process group that uses most of the financial resources, and can result in "rolling wave"

Copyright © Mometrix Media. You have been licensed one copy of this document for personal use only. Any other reproduction or redistribution is strictly prohibited. All rights reserved.

changes to the Initiating and Planning Processes. Its subgroups are:

- Direct and Manage Project Execution – performs the work of the project or phase.
- Perform Quality Assurance – audit quality requirements and ensure standards.
- Acquire, Develop and Manage Project Team – confirm personnel availability and put the team together; train and develop the team for the tasks at hand; track and manage team performance.
- Distribute Information – to stakeholders.
- Manage Stakeholder Expectations – work with and communicate with all stakeholders, resolving issues as they arise.
- Conduct Procurements – select a vendor based on information collected; award contract(s).

Monitoring and controlling process group

The Monitoring and Controlling Process Group is an ongoing and often concurrent process group that is often the source of updates to other process groups. It tracks, reviews and regulates the progress of the project or phase. Its subgroups are:

- Monitor and Control – measure and track performance; develop forecasts.
- Perform Integrated Change Control – review and approve changes to deliverables, assets, documents, and plan.

- Verify and Control Scope - formalize acceptance of deliverables; monitor status of project scope and manage changes to scope baseline.
- Control Schedule and Cost – manage changes to the schedule and cost baselines.
- Perform Quality Control – analyze results and performance and recommend necessary changes.
- Report Performance – Collect and distribute performance information, measurements and forecasts.
- Monitor and Control Risks – track and monitor risks; implement risk response plans.
- Administer Procurements – management procurement relationships; monitor and revise contracts as needed.

Closing process group

The Closing Process Group finalizes all activities in the other process groups, to formally complete the project or a portion of the project. Its primary steps are:

- Verify acceptance by the end user. Confirm that the project or phase is complete as requested and as delineated in the plan.
- Conduct a review of the end of phase or end of project.
- Record the effects of changing or tailoring any process.
- Document lessons or benefits gained.

Copyright © Mometrix Media. You have been licensed one copy of this document for personal use only. Any other reproduction or redistribution is strictly prohibited. All rights reserved.

- Apply updates as needed to organization process assets such as guidelines and templates.
- Store relevant documents and procedures as archive materials in the Project Management Information System (PMIS).
- Close out all procurements and relevant contracts.

Project integration management

Project Integration Management refers to the coordination of various processes and activities within the Process Groups. It includes unifying the different factors and characteristics, managing stakeholder expectations, making choices about resource allocation, and managing the interrelationship of Process Groups and Knowledge Areas, including the following subgroups:

- Develop Project Charter – develop a document that formally authorizes and project or phase, and documents that it will satisfy stakeholder(s) requirements and expectations.
- Develop Project Management Plan – verify actions needed to define, prepare, and coordinate plans that stem from the Project Charter.
- Direct and Manage Project Execution – implement and perform activities needed and defined to achieve objectives.
- Monitor and Control Project Work – track, review and regulate performance compared to objectives.

- Perform Integrated Change Control – review, approve and manage change requests.
- Close Project or Phase – formally finalize all activities to complete project or phase.

Project charter development

The Inputs of project charter development include:

- A statement of work (SOW) that describes the goals or planned results of the project or phase. It may incorporate business needs or other new requirements of the organization, also details of the product or project to be included, as well as the overall strategic plan of the organization.
- Business Case – an analysis of whether or not the project or product is feasible. The Business Case may be created by an outside stakeholder, and also may include Enterprise Environmental Factors.
- Contract – if a project is being undertaken for an outside entity.
- Enterprise Environmental Factors – such as market demand, organization circumstances, advances in the field, legal requirements or other relevant factors.
- Organizational Process Assets - such as guidelines, templates, and historical information regarding previous projects and products.

Tools and Techniques include expertise and resources from any or all individuals

Copyright © Mometrix Media. You have been licensed one copy of this document for personal use only. Any other reproduction or redistribution is strictly prohibited. All rights reserved.

or groups who can provide valuable input regarding technical or management details. Possible groups or individuals are:

- Other organizational units
- Consultants
- Stakeholders including Customers
- Professional and Technical Associations
- Industry Groups
- Subject Matter Experts
- Project Management Office (PMO)

Project charter outputs include objectives, requirements, schedule, risks, and budget. Project charter outputs encompass and document the needs of the business or customer, and the project or product. The Project Charter should bridge the gap between what the organization and/or stakeholder needs, and the development of the project or product, describing how it will satisfy the needs and how that will be measured. The Project Charter will also document project approval, as well as assign project managers and other responsible individuals.

Project Management Plan development
The Inputs include:

- Project Charter
- Outputs from Planning Processes – Outputs or results from other processes are incorporated and integrated into the Project Plan; therefore they are Inputs to this area of Project Integration. This includes changes and updates to

any aspect or document of the project.

- Enterprise Environmental Factors – including government or industry standards, organization structure and organization information databases, physical facilities and personnel policies.
- Organizational Process Assets – including guidelines, proposal criteria, templates, change control procedures, and historical files on past projects.

Project Integration Management takes in the information, organization parameters, and other process results to incorporate and manage changing information and status throughout the project.

Some of the Tools and Techniques utilized are the resources and expertise needed to:

- Tailor the project to meet specified needs.
- Generate a comprehensive list of details to be included in the project.
- Determine resources and skills or skill levels needed.And delineate project documents needed.
- Determine level of configuration management needed.

Outputs from this process are those characteristics and resources that serve to integrate and consolidate both the baselines and the subsidiary management plans. These characteristics and resources include but are not limited to:

Copyright © Mometrix Media. You have been licensed one copy of this document for personal use only. Any other reproduction or redistribution is strictly prohibited. All rights reserved.

- Determination of a life cycle for the project and its respective phases.
- How work will be performed to meet project objectives.
- How configuration management will be performed.
- Communication plan with stakeholders.
- How integrity of the baselines will be maintained.

Project execution direction and management

Project Execution Direction and Management refer to performance of the activities needed to accomplish the project or phase. In cooperation with the management team, the Project Manager directs the relevant activities and manages the interfacing of the different activities and factors within the project. Relevant activities include but are not limited to:

- Those performed to meet the requirements.
- Creating project deliverables.
- Staffing and training of human resources.
- Establishing and managing communication channels.
- Implementing methods and standards.
- Managing risks.
- Issuing change requests and adapting project variables as appropriate.
- Managing sellers and suppliers.

- Collecting and documenting learned lessons to be later referred to and applied.

Part of project execution is also collection and documentation of work performance information that will become an input to the Monitor and Control Process.

Inputs include:
- Project Management Plan
- Approved Change Requests – Once a change request has been approved, it becomes the input for the execution of modifying project variables as indicated.
- Enterprise Environmental Factors – include company culture and structure, personnel and personnel administration, facilities and infrastructure, information systems, as well as stakeholder risk tolerances.
- Organizational Process Assets – include standard guidelines and procedures, the communication environment, issue and defect policies/practices, measurement databases, management information from previous projects, also issue and defect management databases.

Tools and Techniques include:
- Expertise and Consultancy Resources – from other units within the organization, consultants, stakeholders including customers or sponsors, also professional and technical associations.

Copyright © Mometrix Media. You have been licensed one copy of this document for personal use only. Any other reproduction or redistribution is strictly prohibited. All rights reserved.

- Project Management Information System – is an input as one of the enterprise environmental factors, but it is also a tool in that it can provide access to software for scheduling, etc., as well as databases for configuration management, information collection, etc.

Outputs include:
- Deliverables – product, result or capability
- Work Performance Information – such as status of deliverable(s) or schedule, also costs incurred.
- Project management plan updates to such variables as requirements, schedule, cost, quality management, human resources, communications, risk management and baselines.
- Project Documentation Updates regarding such variables as requirements, risk and stakeholder registers.

Another type of Output is Change Requests, which may be initiated either internally or externally, and modifies procedures, scope, cost/budget, schedule, or project quality. They may also address:
- Corrective Action – to bring the project in line with the project management plan.
- Preventive Action – reduces the effect of existing and potential risks.
- Defect Repair – identify defect and recommend action to rectify.

- Updates – modifications to documents or plans to reflect changes.

Project Integration Change Control Process

A basic project management plan can be either summarized or detailed, and may include one or more subsidiary, or sub-plans. Each sub-plan can contain details about that specific phase or the project, and may impact or be impacted by other sub-plans. The Project Integration Change Control Process endeavors to coordinate the changing and interrelated details of all the sub-plans and how they may change the baseline categories. Pertinent baseline categories are:
- Schedule, cost, scope and their respective management plans

Project Integration Management works with subsidiary management plans for at least the following categories:
- Scope
- Schedule
- Cost
- Quality
- Personnel/Staff
- Risk Management
- Communications Management
- Procurement Management.

Integrated Change Control involves reviewing, approving and managing change requests, throughout the life of the project. Includes the following:
- Ensures that only approved changes are released and implemented. Responsibly

Copyright © Mometrix Media. You have been licensed one copy of this document for personal use only. Any other reproduction or redistribution is strictly prohibited. All rights reserved.

reviews and approves/denies change requests expediently.

- Coordinates changes across the entire project.
- Documents the effect of changes to plans and baselines.
- Tracks all changes and change requests.
- Oversees the ongoing need for changes to plans and baselines. Continuously communicates changes to stakeholders or others as needed.

Inputs include:
- Project Management Plan
- Work Performance Information
- Enterprise Environmental Factors – information collection and distribution systems and databases, etc.
- Organizational Process Assets – Change control procedures and databases, project files.

Tools and Techniques include expertise and consultancy resources from consultants, stakeholders, professional associations, subject matter experts, and project management office. Outputs include Status Updates for Change Requests, and Management Plan Updates.

Monitoring and Controlling

Monitoring and Controlling involves collecting, measuring, assessing and distributing information of the project. Its areas of concern include: comparing progress and performance against the plan, determining if new actions need to be implemented, identifying and tracking

new risks, accurately maintaining an information and document database, or providing forecasts. Monitoring changes.

Inputs include:
- Project Management Plan. Performance Reports – regarding status, accomplishments, schedule, forecasts, etc.
- Enterprise Environmental Factors – standards, organizational processes, stakeholder risk tolerances, and relevant databases. Organizational Process Assets – communication practices, financial procedures, defect and risk management procedures, and lessons learned databases.

Tools/Techniques are the collective expertise of the management team in interpreting information generated in the process.

Closing Project or Phase

In Project Integration Management, closing a project or phase refers to finalizing all activities across all process groups, ensuring completion against the project management plan. This phase also establishes the process for investigation and recourse if the project/phase is closed prematurely. The process includes:
- Actions that complete or satisfy exit criteria
- Actions needed to transfer the results/output to the next phase and/or to production.

Copyright © Mometrix Media. You have been licensed one copy of this document for personal use only. Any other reproduction or redistribution is strictly prohibited. All rights reserved.

- Activities to collect records and assess project/phase success or failure.

Inputs include:
- Project management plan
- Accepted deliverables - product, result or capability
- Organizational process assets – such as closure guidelines and databases of documents and lessons learned.

Tools and Techniques include expert judgment to ensure closure procedures adhere to standards.

Outputs include:
- Final product, service or transition
- Updates to organizational process assets – including documents, project files, and lessons learned information.

Project scope management

Project Scope Management refers primarily to determining and managing the activities and processes required for the project completion, including making sure that only those needed for the project or product is included. Main areas of concern, or processes, include:
- Collect requirements: defining and documenting stakeholder needs.
- Developing a detailed description of the project or product.

- Subdividing deliverables into more manageable components.
- Verifying and confirming acceptance of the project deliverables.
- Monitoring the status of the project or product scope.
- Managing changes to the scope baseline.

These are broad categories of process that may be sequential or concurrent, and may overlap and interact.

Collecting requirements

Collecting Requirements is essentially defining and managing customer/stakeholder needs and expectations. Specifically, it details the requirements of stakeholders through a process of capturing, analyzing and recording the information. Requirements should be quantified – giving numerical information for analysis – and documented or recorded. These details form the basis for cost, schedule and quality planning. They may also be divided between project requirements and product requirements. Requirement details may address requirements for business, delivery, project management, etc. Requirements can also include information such as technical or security requirements.
Inputs include:
- Project Charter – providing the level and detail needed for managing project scope.
- Stakeholder Register – to identify stakeholders than can provide details needed.

Copyright © Mometrix Media. You have been licensed one copy of this document for personal use only. Any other reproduction or redistribution is strictly prohibited. All rights reserved.

The tools and techniques are:
- Interviews – focusing on group consultancy and collective expertise. This can be augmented by interviews with experienced stakeholders or relevant experts.
- Focus Groups – using a trained facilitator to lead the group in a focused, interactive discussion. Groups should include pertinent stakeholders and/or relevant experts.
- Creativity Techniques – such as brainstorming, nominal group technique, the
- Delphi technique, idea mapping, and affinity diagrams.
- Group Decision-Making Techniques – such as unanimity, majority, plurality, or dictatorship, which are different methods for coming to a conclusion about the scope of the project or product.
- Questionnaires or Surveys.
- Observations.
- Prototypes – which provide early feedback by using a working model of the expected product.

Following are the outputs for collecting requirements:
- Requirements Documentation – addressing how requirements meet the needs of the project. Requirements must be measurable, testable, traceable, complete, consistent, and acceptable to stakeholders. It may grow in detail as more

information is acquired. Should include peripheral information such as level of service, security and compliance requirements. It should also address potential impacts to other areas or departments.
- Requirements Management Plan – documents how requirements will be analyzed, recorded and managed throughout the project. Should also address how changes will be managed, how impacts will be analyzed and which details should be traced and how.
- Requirements Traceability Matrix – the format is usually a table that links requirements to the business and project objective and tracks them throughout the project life cycle.

Defining scope
Defining scope implies a level of detail and analysis that is pivotal to the success of the project. It includes:
- Detailed description of the project or product
- Analysis of existing and potential risks

Inputs include:
- Project Charter. Requirements Documentation
- Organizational Process Assets – guidelines and templates related to project scope statements, files and lessons learned from previous projects.

Tools and techniques include:

- 19 -

Copyright © Mometrix Media. You have been licensed one copy of this document for personal use only.
Any other reproduction or redistribution is strictly prohibited. All rights reserved.

- Expert Judgment - from consultants, stakeholders, professional groups, subject matter experts and other units in the organization.
- Product Analysis – translating product description into tangible deliverables.
- Alternatives Identification – a variety of brainstorming. Workshops

Outputs are the Project Scope Statement which includes:

- Project Scope Description
- Project Acceptance Criteria
- Project Deliverables
- Project Exclusions – what is excluded from the project.
- Project Constraints – how the scope is limited.
- Project Document Updates - may impact the stakeholder register, requirements documentation, and the traceability matrix.

Work Breakdown Structure

The idea of a Work Breakdown Structure, WBS, is precisely to break down the deliverables into smaller, more manageable parts. It is generally organized into increasingly detailed levels, broken down into singular tasks. For instance, if the task is to schedule the entire project, a WBS would assess the time needed for each subsequent component of the project, and add them together for a total schedule needed. Another WBS might be to determine cost of a completed product by first

determining costs of each component, combined with cost of manufacture. Inputs include:

- Project Scope Statement
- Requirements Documentation
- Organizational Process Assets – including policies and procedures for WBS, also project files and lessons learned from previous projects.

Tools and Techniques are essential decomposition, which is the actual process of subdividing the work into more management components. It includes: Identifying, organizing, decomposing into elements, assigning codes to the elements, and monitoring/ensuring that the level of decomposition breakdown is necessary.

Outputs include:

- The WBS - a formalized decomposition of the work, including control accounts for the work groups, or packages, as well as identifiers for components of the work.
- WBS Dictionary – cross-reference matching work components with unique identifiers. Should at least contain a code, a description of what that code describes a viable organizational scheme, as well as specifics such as cost, schedule, etc.
- Scope Baseline – a component of the management plan, which includes the Scope Statement, the WBS, and the WBS Dictionary.
- Project Document Updates

Copyright © Mometrix Media. You have been licensed one copy of this document for personal use only. Any other reproduction or redistribution is strictly prohibited. All rights reserved.

Verifying Scope

Verifying Scope refers to confirming, or validating the project scope with the customer or sponsor. It provides formalized acceptance of the scope of the project.

Its Inputs include:

- Project Management Plan – including the Scope Statement, the WBS and the WBS Dictionary.
- Requirements Documentation – This should list all the project, product, technical requirements, etc.
- Traceability Matrix
- Validated Deliverables – which have been completed and checked for correctness by the Perform Quality Control Process.

The primary Tool and Technique is inspection, which includes measuring, examining, etc. to ensure the product meets the acceptance criteria.

Outputs include:

- Accepted Deliverables – notice this is different than *acceptable*. They have to have been accepted.
- Change Requests – generated if deliverables are not accepted.
- Project Document Updates

Controlling Scope

Controlling Scope refers to an ongoing process of monitoring the baseline scope of the project, including change requests. Controlling scope includes ensuring that change requests are implemented and then integrating those changes into the scope.

Its Inputs include:

- Project Management Plan(s) – scope baseline and scope, change, requirement and configuration management
- Work Performance Information
- Requirements Documentation and Traceability Matrix
- Organizational Process Assets – including monitoring and reporting procedures

Tools and Techniques refer generally to variance analysis. Outputs include:

- Work Performance Measurements
- Organizational Process Assess Updates – causes of variances, corrective actions, lessons learned, etc.
- Change Requests
- Project Management Plan Updates – to scope and other baselines
- Project Document Updates

Project time management

Project Time Management refers to the activities and processes that contribute to timely completion of the project--usually a concerted effort by the project management team. Activities are documented and recorded. They include Defining Activities, Sequence Activities, Estimating Activity, Developing and Controlling Schedule.

Defining Activities

Defining Activities identifies specific actions to product the product deliverables. Actions include estimates

Copyright © Mometrix Media. You have been licensed one copy of this document for personal use only. Any other reproduction or redistribution is strictly prohibited. All rights reserved.

for scheduling, executing, monitoring and controlling the project.

Its Inputs include:

- Scope Baseline
- Enterprise Environmental Factors such as existing information systems
- Organizational Process Assets – guidelines and templates for guidelines and lessons learned.

Tools and Techniques for Defining Activities include:

- Decomposition – subdividing the project into activities
- Rolling Wave Planning – current activities are more detailed; future activities are more generally planned.
- Templates – from previous projects.
- Expert Judgment – people or groups with expertise in project scheduling.

Outputs include Activity Lists, Activity Attributes identifying components, and Milestone Lists indicating completion of specific goals or phases.

Sequencing Activities

Sequencing Activities refers to identifying and documenting activities, and developing a sequence. Each activity logically follows the one preceding it. Its Inputs include the Activity List, Activity Attributes, and Milestone List – Outputs from Defining Activities. Its Tools and Techniques include:

- Precedence Diagramming Method (PDM) – precise method of

diagramming project schedules using graphics such as boxes and arrows to represent activities and the relationship between activities. These generally fall into the categories of finish to start (FS), finish to finish (FF), start to start (SS), and start to finish (SF).
- Dependency Determination – broken into categories of 1) Mandatory or predetermined by the team, 2) Discretionary or decided during the project, and External or depending on external factors.
- Applying Leads and Lags – starting a sequenced activity early (lead) or late (lag).

Its Outputs include:

- Project Schedule Network Diagrams – graphic displays of the schedule activities and sequence relationships.
- Project Document Updates – updating Activity Lists, Activity Attributes, and/or Risk Register.

Estimating Activity Resources

Estimating Activity Resources refers to those people, equipment, supplies, etc. needed to perform or complete an activity. Its Inputs include the Activity List, Activity Attributes, and Resource Calendars—indicating availability of resources, such as people needed for the project and their available hours. Other inputs are Enterprise Environmental Factors such as available skills, also Organizational Process Assets such as

Copyright © Mometrix Media. You have been licensed one copy of this document for personal use only. Any other reproduction or redistribution is strictly prohibited. All rights reserved.

staffing and purchasing policies, as well as historical information on resources.
Its Tools and Techniques include:

- Expert Judgment - regarding resources
- Alternative Analysis – back-up plans regarding resources
- Published Estimating Data – available data on estimating
- Bottom-Up Estimating – a type of decomposition estimating that breaks down into activities, and considers external and other time-affecting factors.
- Project Management Software

Outputs include Activity Resource Requirements specifying types and quantities of resources needed, also Resource Breakdown Structure, a prioritized listing of resources such as labor, material, equipment, etc.

Estimating Activity Durations
Estimating Activity Durations is the process of estimating the amount of time each activity will take. The process is an ongoing one throughout the project, incorporating new input from previously completed activities or other factors. The estimates apply to the amount of work effort as well as the amount of durations needed for each activity. Its Inputs include:

- Activity List
- Activity Attributes
- Activity Resource Requirements
- Resource Calendars - resource availability will affect duration.

- Project Scope Statement – including constraints and assumptions from the Statement. Factors to consider include existing conditions, availability of information, availability of resources, contract terms.
- Enterprise Environmental Factors – estimating databases, productivity metrics and published commercial information.
- Organizational Process Assets – relevant historical information, project calendars, scheduling processes, and lessons learned.

Tools and Techniques of estimating activity durations include:

- Expertise and Historical Information
- Analogous Estimating – using information about complexity, duration, etc. from a similar, previous project.
- Parametric Estimating – using historical information factored by other variables such as size constraints.
- Three-Point Estimates – most the Program Evaluation and Review Technique (PERT) to approximate the duration of a project using estimates for most likely (m), optimistic (o), or pessimistic (p). The PERT estimate uses a weighted average of m, o, and p.
- Reserve Analysis – assessing contingency reserves, which may change as the activities unfold.

- 23 -

Copyright © Mometrix Media. You have been licensed one copy of this document for personal use only. Any other reproduction or redistribution is strictly prohibited. All rights reserved.

Outputs include:
- Activity Duration Estimates – usually numerical in nature, a range of possible least and most duration, and not including lags.
- Project Documents Updates – possibly estimates of Activity Attributes and of skill levels and availability.

Developing Schedule

Developing Schedule, particularly in terms of Project Time Management, is an ongoing process that requires oversight and periodic revisions to reflect changes in resources or other scheduling factors. In other words, project time management involves looking at each portion of the schedule—each activity and its proposed duration—and adjusting it as new information comes into play. Its components include activity sequences and durations. It incorporates resource requirements and constraints such as supplies, personnel, etc. Within the context of Project Time Management, schedule development and maintenance is a baseline component for other areas of management. Its Inputs include:
- Activity List
- Activity Attributes
- Project Schedule Network Diagrams
- Activity Resource Requirements
- Resource Calendars
- Activity Duration Estimates
- Project Scope Statement
- Enterprise Environmental Factors – such as a scheduling tool

- Organizational Process Assets

Tools and Techniques include: Scheduling Network Analysis – using Critical Path Method, Critical Chain Method, What If Analysis, and Resource Leveling. Critical Path Method – calculating early and late start and finish dates. Critical Chain Method – accounting for factors that could alter schedule, and adding in buffers at critical points in the schedule. Resource Leveling – takes into account resources that are shared during critical times, or unavailable during certain parts of the schedule. What-If Analysis – developing alternate action or schedule plans based on the possibility of a contingency such as reduced resources or other factors that can affect the schedule. Applying Leads and Lags. Schedule Compression – shortens the project without changing the project scope. May including tradeoffs between cost and schedule (Crashing), or running activities parallel instead of sequential (Fast Tracking).

Outputs include: Project Schedule – including start and finish dates for each activity. Also should reflect resource avail-ability. Can be represented using milestone charts, bar charts and project schedule network diagrams. Schedule Baseline. Schedule Data – including milestones, activity duration and attributes, identified assumptions and constraints. Project Document Updates – possibly including updates to re-source requirements, activity attributes, calendar and risk register.

- 24 -

Copyright © Mometrix Media. You have been licensed one copy of this document for personal use only. Any other reproduction or redistribution is strictly prohibited. All rights reserved.

Controlling Schedule

Controlling Schedule in terms of Project Time Management relates to oversight and monitoring of the schedule including:

- Determining the current schedule status.
- Recognizing factors that can affect the schedule.
- Identifying and managing changes as they occur.

Its Inputs include:

- Project Management Plan – in terms of scheduling
- Project Schedule. Work Performance Information – tracking status of work activities
- Organizational Process Assets – such as schedule control policies, tools, and reporting methods

Its Tools and Techniques include:

- Performance Reviews - which measure, compare and analyze schedule performance. A complex process that compares schedule, resources, constraints, and activity status, and determines if factors affect the schedule enough to make significant changes to the baseline.
- Variance Analysis – looking at variations to the schedule baseline
- Project Management Software
- Resource Leveling. What-If Scenario Analysis
- Adjusting Leads and Lags. Schedule Compressions
- Scheduling Tools

Outputs include:

- Work Performance Measurements – such as Schedule Variance (SV), and Schedule Performance Index (SPI). Measurements are recorded to communicate to stakeholders.
- Updates to Organizational Process Assets – such as causes for change, actions related to change, lessons learned.
- Change Requests – schedule variances as appropriate, which may be a reaction to changes in the schedule, or may be preventive action to alleviate negative variances in the future.
- Management Plan Updates – including schedule and cost baselines, and the schedule management plan itself.
- Project Document Updates – including schedule data such as diagrams, or a complete reworking of the project schedule or its individual activity components.
- Project Schedule – a change to the actual schedule or its components.

Project cost management

Project Cost Management is concerned with both controlling and estimating costs, within a determined budget. The process involves estimating costs within particular work components such as activities within the work breakdown structure (WBS). It is not a one-time endeavor, but rather occurs throughout the project, and for particular phases or

Copyright © Mometrix Media. You have been licensed one copy of this document for personal use only. Any other reproduction or redistribution is strictly prohibited. All rights reserved.

portions of the project. Its component concerns are:

- Project Scope Statement
- Determining a level of accuracy
- Determining units of measure
- Developing a framework for estimating
- Applying a quantitative weight to performance measurements
- Deciding on reporting formats of information and estimates
- Clearly documenting and reporting on the three basic components of estimating costs, determining the budget, and controlling costs.
- Controlling thresholds

Level of accuracy

Determining a level of accuracy refers to including how to round cost estimates—to the nearest thousand dollars, hundred dollars, etc., in relation to the overall budget and size of the project. Determining units of measure refers to developing a consistent unit of measurement for items such as staff availability—measured by hours, or days, or weeks, for instance. Developing a framework for estimating is based around the WBS. This means that the cost estimating should relate directly to the work units, so that each phase, or other component, of the project is assigned a specific code and then a cost is estimated and identified accordingly.

Quantitative weight

Applying a quantitative weight to performance measurements is a way of determining how important a phase, a factor, or a variance is, and applying a numerical weight to it. For instance, if a phase budget is $100,000 and it includes mostly labor, then the availability and performance of staff is extremely important and should be given a higher numerical value when estimating Reporting information and estimates involves determining a reporting format, such as numerical graphs, also clearly documenting and reporting on the three basic components of estimating costs, determining the budget, and controlling costs. Controlling variance thresholds means determining and managing an agreed-upon threshold for variances such as staff resources, to determine if cost estimating will be affected. For instance, if a project involves mostly concrete, it means determining how much the price of concrete can be before it affects the cost of the project.

Estimating costs

Estimating costs, in terms of Project Cost Management, is a complex, ongoing process that involves determining a predicted cost of a project, a phase, or other component, based on information received. Estimates will be more and more detailed, and more and more accurate as the project or phase progresses, and estimates should indicate a degree of accuracy accordingly. In other words, an early estimate might be off by more or less 40%, whereas an revised estimate that is closer to the end date of the project phase would probably be accurate more or less 10%. Estimates are determined and revised according to much of the information that is Output

Copyright © Mometrix Media. You have been licensed one copy of this document for personal use only. Any other reproduction or redistribution is strictly prohibited. All rights reserved.

information from other processes. It is essentially assigning a monetary amount to time, resources, staffing, etc., and managing that estimate according to the status of the job and any variations in the factors affecting costs. Includes trade-off and other contingency estimates.

Cost estimates can be either for just direct costs such as material used, or also for indirect costs such as having to send photocopying to an outside source while the photocopy room is being remodeled. The Inputs include:

- Project Scope Baseline – description of the project as well as its boundaries and constraints such as legal requirements, acceptance criteria, etc.
- Work Breakdown Structure – including the WBS dictionary – to estimate costs related to each work unit.
- Project Schedule – incorporating factors such as activity duration and cost variances related to duration, such as paying overtime if required.
- Human Resource Information – such as pay rates for particular skills, etc.
- Risk Register – assessing which risks are likely to have an impact on cost estimating.
- Enterprise Environmental Factors – such as marketing conditions for resources, and other externally determined factors.
- Organizational Process Assets – such as cost estimating policies, templates, and lessons learned.

Tools and Techniques of estimating costs include:

- Expert Judgment – which in this case refers more to historical information than expertise, although it can include the ability to interpret that information such as labor rates, material costs, inflation, etc.
- Analogous Estimating – estimating that incorporates and aggregates such factors as cost, duration, variance thresholds, etc., to estimate as accurately as possible.
- Parametric Estimating – looking at the parameters such as square footage incorporated with historical data such as how much concrete is generally used for a certain amount of square footage.
- Three-Point Estimating – estimating based on likelihood, such as the likelihood of weather being a factor in estimating.
- Reserve Analysis – including estimates for back-up or contingency resources if needed.
- Cost of Quality
- Estimating Software
- Vendor Bid Analysis – taking critical look at what supply vendors are bidding against what supplies or other resources should cost.

Outputs of Estimating Costs include:

- Activity Cost Estimates – generally direct cost estimates such as

Copyright © Mometrix Media. You have been licensed one copy of this document for personal use only. Any other reproduction or redistribution is strictly prohibited. All rights reserved.

material, equipment, etc., for each work activity.

- Basis of Estimates – documentation of what factors went into the estimate, such as how the estimate was determined, what constraints and other considerations were included, and how they were estimated.

Determining Budget refers to a reasonable totaling of all estimated costs to determine a reasonable or projected budget. This is compared to the authorized budget to further refine the budget based on estimated costs. Its Inputs include:

- Activity Cost Estimates
- Basis of Estimates
- Scope Baseline
- Project Schedule
- Resource Calendars
- Contracts
- Organizational Process Assets

Tools and Techniques of determining budget include:

- Cost Aggregation – aggregating costs of individual project components such as work packages to project costs of larger components such as phases or projects.
- Reserve Analysis – allowances for changes or risk factors. Includes management reserve allowances.
- Expert Judgment – stakeholders, consultants, other units, etc., providing expertise regarding cost estimates.

- Historical Relationships – for instance, estimating the cost of paper for a printing project incorporating a climbing paper cost percentage per month, times the number of months estimated for the project.
- Funding Limit Reconciliation – revising cost estimates based on the availability of a certain type of funds, or period of time of availability.

Outputs of determining budget include:

- Cost Performance Baseline – a time/cost graph culminating budget at completion (BAC), incorporating funding limits, cost estimates, and performance status.
- Project Funding Requirements – looking at both total funding and periodic funding requirements, incorporating funding limits as applicable.

Controlling costs

Controlling costs refers just as much to monitoring as it does to controlling. It includes looking at funds expended vis-à-vis work performed, and making recommendations if there is a disparity. It also includes monitoring the projected budget against the actual expenditures, and making adjustments if needed. Adjustments may be to revise the estimate, or may be to curtail expenditures. It includes isolating and analyzing variances and making recommendations—for instance, if the cost of paper goes up unexpectedly,

Copyright © Mometrix Media. You have been licensed one copy of this document for personal use only. Any other reproduction or redistribution is strictly prohibited. All rights reserved.

controlling costs may mean an adjusted cost estimate. It also means ensuring that only approved changes are implemented, and also that approved relevant changes are communicated to stakeholders. Its Inputs include:

- Project Management Plan
- Project Funding Requirements
- Work Performance Information – such as status of deliverables and costs incurred so far.
- Organizational Process Assets – such as cost control policies and tools, and monitoring and reporting methods used.

Tools and techniques of controlling costs include:

- Earned Value Management (EVM) – measures work performed using planned value or authorized budget, earned value or budget assigned to a component, and actual cost.
- Monitoring Schedule and Cost Variances
- Converting Variances - to schedule performance index (SPI) or cost performance index (CPI).
- Forecasting – Estimate at Completion (EAC) versus Budget at Completion (BAC). EAC looks at expenditures so far, and then estimates or extrapolates how much to complete – Estimate to Completion (ETC)
- T0-Complete Performance Index – a calculated projection of cost performance that must be achieved on the remaining work

to meet a specific management goal.

- Performance Reviews – periodic cost analyses as work progresses, incorporating variance analysis, trend analysis, and earned value performance.
- Variance Analysis
- Project Management Software

Outputs related to Project Cost Management cost control include:

- Work Performance Measurements – specifically values for WBS components representing cost and schedule variances, and cost and schedule performance indices.
- Budget Forecasts
- Organizational Process Updates – causes of variances, and/or corrective actions taken.
- Change Requests
- Project Management Plan Updates
- Project Document Updates

Project quality management

Project Quality Management refers to the policies, practices and procedures that monitor and oversee that the project meets the requirements and needs that were originally intended. It encompasses both the management and the performance of the work, and covers all phases and components of the project. Management areas include overall Plan Quality, Quality Assurance and Quality Control.

Copyright © Mometrix Media. You have been licensed one copy of this document for personal use only. Any other reproduction or redistribution is strictly prohibited. All rights reserved.

Project Quality Management monitors both quality, and the assurance that the product meets the requirement, as well as grade, which refers to level of performance and/or issues of defect. It also monitors precision, which refers to the consistency of repeated measurements, as well as accuracy, which means that the measured value is very close to the true value. Project Quality Management also focuses on:

- Customer Satisfaction
- Prevention over Inspection – foreseeing and correcting problems well before the inspection phase
- Continuous Improvement – using the plan-do-check-act cycle.
- Providing Leadership and Resources

Plan Quality

Plan Quality is the umbrella process of determining what constitutes quality of the management plan including requirements and standards that can be documented to validate that the project is compliant with its goals. Its Inputs include:

- Scope Baseline – including major project deliverables and acceptance criteria, as well as work breakdown structure and dictionary of WBS elements.
- Stakeholder Register
- Cost Performance Baseline
- Schedule Baseline
- Risk Register
- Enterprise Environmental Factors – regulations, standards and guidelines as well as working conditions that could impact quality
- Organizational Process Assets – policies, procedures and guidelines related to quality as well as lessons learned in that area. Communicate to stakeholders and other as appropriate the source of quality policy – whether industry, organizational, etc.

Tools and Techniques of plan quality include:

- Cost-Benefit Analysis – benefits compared to cost of those benefits. Cost of Quality (COQ)
- Control Charts – monitor output variables, tracking maximum and minimum allowed values.
- Benchmarking. Design of Experiments (DOE) – quantitative analysis of which factors may affect process or product variables. Statistical Sampling - quality sampling of a project or product, such as 10 bicycles in a production line of 200 bicycles. Flowchart – of different processes or actions, and the relationships between them. Proprietary Quality Management Methodologies – include Six Sigma, Lean Six Sigma, Quality Function Deployment, etc. Analytical Methodologies – such as brainstorming, diagrams, etc.

Outputs include:

- Quality Management Plan

Copyright © Mometrix Media. You have been licensed one copy of this document for personal use only. Any other reproduction or redistribution is strictly prohibited. All rights reserved.

- Quality Metrics – numerical definitions of how quality standards will be measured including allowable variations
- Quality Checklists – delineating quality plan(s) for specific components
- Process Improvement Plan – processes and steps involved in the quality plan
- Project Document Updates – including stakeholder register and responsibility assignment matrix.

Quality assurance

Performing Quality Assurance is a matter of monitoring adherence to quality policies and standards. Its Inputs include:
- Project Management Plan – including quality management and process improvement plans
- Quality Metrics
- Work Performance Information – such as technical measurements, deliverables status, schedule progress and costs incurred
- Quality Control Measurements

Its Tools and Techniques include:
- Quality Audits – looking at best practices and at shortcomings. Also includes communicating findings and offering assistance to rectify shortcomings or encourage good practices.
- Process Analysis – follows steps in Process Improvement Plan

Outputs include:

- Organizational Process Assets Updates
- Change Requests
- Project Management Plan Updates – to quality, schedule and cost management as indicated
- Product Document Updates – to quality audit reports, training plans, and process documentation

Quality control

Performing Quality Control refers to monitoring and recording quality assurance activities, and recommending changes as appropriate. It looks at standards related to deliverables as well as cost or schedule performance. Key focus terms are:
- Prevention – preventing errors in the process
- Inspection – preventing errors from reaching the customer
- Attribute Sampling – whether or not a product sampling conforms to standards
- Variable Sampling – measures the degree of conformity
- Tolerances – specified range of acceptable results – and Control Limits

Its Inputs include:
- Project Management Plan
- Quality Metrics
- Quality Checklists
- Work Performance Measurements – comparing technical, schedule, and cost plans against actual performance
- Approved Change Requests

Copyright © Mometrix Media. You have been licensed one copy of this document for personal use only. Any other reproduction or redistribution is strictly prohibited. All rights reserved.

- Deliverables
- Organizational Process Assets – such as quality standards and policies, standard work guidelines, and issue and defect reporting policies

Tools and Techniques include:
- Cause and Effect or Ishikawa Diagrams – organizational diagrams linking variables with outcomes.
- Charts - such as control charts which look at acceptability of variances, flowcharts which look at relationships between processes, histograms which are a bar chart tracing how a variable or problem occurred, Pareto charts which rank causes by number of effects, run charts which show a history and pattern of variation, and scatter charts which show the relationship between two variables.
- Trend Analysis – monitoring scheduling, cost and performance analysis.
- Inspection
- Approved Change Requests Review

Outputs include:
- Quality Control Measurements – documented results
- Validated Changes – inspected, then accepted or rejected
- Validated Variables

- Organizational Process Assets – such as completed checklists, and lessons learned documentation
- Change Requests
- Project Management Plan Updates – to quality management plan and/or process improvement plan
- Project Document Updates – including quality standards

Project human resource management

Project Human Resource Management encompasses leading and organizing the Project Team—people involved in a project. The management team is a part of the project team, and is specifically responsible for initiation, planning, executing, monitoring, controlling and closing the various project phases. The project team is not a static group of people, and may change in relation to phases or status of the project. Human resource management includes incorporating factors that can influence team performance such as organizational culture, communication among stakeholders, internal and external politics, geographic factors, etc. Human resource management also means managing the project team's ethical and professional behavior where applicable. The main components of Project Human Resource Management are:
- Developing a Human Resource Plan
- Acquiring a Project Team
- Developing a Project Team
- Managing the Project Team

Developing a human resource plan

- 32 -

Copyright © Mometrix Media. You have been licensed one copy of this document for personal use only. Any other reproduction or redistribution is strictly prohibited. All rights reserved.

Developing a Human Resource Plan is a comprehensive process that first begins with identifying the roles, responsibilities and skills needed to complete a project. This is further detailed by matching skill levels and availability of current employees, and/or training needed to develop skills if needed. For long-term projects, it may include team building and reward strategies. It may also be necessary to hire from outside the organization to obtain the necessary skills, or to cover employees other tasks while they are devoted to a project. The Human Resource Plan also may impact schedule, cost, and other baselines. Its Inputs include:

- Activity Resource Requirements – number of people/hours as well as competencies
- Enterprise Environmental Factors – including organizational culture, current employees, personnel administration policies and marketplace conditions
- Organizational Process Assets – policies, procedures, guidelines, templates and historical information related to human resources.

Tools and Techniques include:

- Organizational Charts – examples include hierarchical, which show responsibilities under high-level roles such as department managers, matrix-based, which shows activities connected to each person, with only one person connected to one activity, and text-oriented, which give a brief narration under a person and his/her role or activity.
- Organizational Breakdown Structure (OBS) – a component of a hierarchical chart
- Networking – activities that formally or informally gather information about political and interpersonal factors that impact human resource management.
- Organizational Theory

Outputs include:

- Human Resource Plan – including roles and responsibilities, organizational charts, clear delineation of authority, project organization charts, and staffing management plans.
- Staffing Management Plan – includes staff acquisition, resource calendars, staff release plan, training needs, plans for recognition and rewards, strategies for compliance with regulations, and safety policies and procedures.

Acquiring a project team
Acquiring a project team involves first determining the number of people and competencies needed to complete a project, then determining the availability of those people and competencies, and acting accordingly. If the number of people and/or competencies is not available – due to other organizational priorities, or external factors – the project team still needs to be acquired; Human Resource Management may entail revising and providing alternate

- 33 -

Copyright © Mometrix Media. You have been licensed one copy of this document for personal use only. Any other reproduction or redistribution is strictly prohibited. All rights reserved.

strategies to best acquire the human resources necessary. It also may involve negotiating with other departments to acquire the people necessary, such as offering clerical assistance while "borrowing" someone from the department to work on a particular project. Its Inputs include:

- Project Management Plan – including needed competencies and responsibilities, and time periods needed for each.
- Enterprise Environmental Factors – such as availability, human resource policies, organizational structure or location
- Organizational Process Assets – policies, procedures, guidelines

Tools and techniques of acquiring a project team include:

- Pre-assignment – assignment of someone to be on the project that has been previously agreed upon.
- Negotiation – with team members, with other project teams, and possibly with outside vendors, to obtain necessary human resources and "buy-in" from their respective departments or agencies.
- Acquisition – possibly from outside sources
- Virtual Teams – reducing the need for people to travel, or to spend time in a specific location, by being available electronically.

Outputs include:

- Project Staff Assignments – clear delineation of who is doing what;

may include a project team directory
- Resource Calendars – documents time period that each team member can work on the project
- Project Management Plan Updates

Developing a project team

Developing a Project Team refers to creating and enhancing the team competencies and dynamics once the team has been acquired. It includes training team members in the knowledge and skills necessary to do the job. It also includes creating a work environment that encourages open communication, develops trust among its members, and promotes the kind of interdependent working environment that will sustain a strong level of team participation throughout the project or phase. Team development may include trust exercises and/or reward systems. Its Inputs include:

- Project Staff Assignments
- Project Management Plan
- Resource Calendars

Its Outputs include:

- Team Performance Assessments – noting and reporting improvements in skills, reduced staff turnover, and success in reaching goals.
- Recommendations for Team Improvement – should be well documented and take culture and legalities into account
- Enterprise Environmental Factors Updates – such as employee training records

- 34 -

Copyright © Mometrix Media. You have been licensed one copy of this document for personal use only. Any other reproduction or redistribution is strictly prohibited. All rights reserved.

Tools and Techniques for Developing a Project Team include:

- Interpersonal Skills – including sensitivity, empathy, creativity and group facilitation
- Training – as indicated, to enhance team member skills
- Team-Building Activities – for managing and reducing the occurrence of conflict throughout the five stages of team development: forming, storming (addressing the work at hand), norming (becoming more familiar with each other), performing and adjourning.
- Ground Rules – establish clear expectations.
- Co-Location – bringing team members physically together
- Recognition and Rewards – recommended throughout the project

Managing a Project Team

Managing a Project Team refers to assessing team performance, providing feedback to the team members, resolving issues, and managing changes. It is the actions that stem from the overview of team management.

Inputs include:

- Project Staff Assignments. Project Management Plan – including roles, organization, and staffing plans.
- Performance Reports – indicating project status compared to project forecasts and any need for increasing performance

effectiveness. Organizational Process Assets – such as certificates of appreciation, bonus structures, newsletters, websites, corporate apparel and other reward possibilities.

Tools and Techniques include:

- Observation and Conversation. Constructive Performance Appraisals. Conflict Management – focusing on current issues, the importance of the conflict and possible ramifications.
- Conflict Resolution Techniques – avoidance, accommodating, compromising, forcing, collaborating, and confronting/problem solving. Issue Log – including a target date for resolution
- Interpersonal Skills – active listening, persuasive skills, critical information gathering, effective decision making, etc.

Outputs include:

- Enterprise Environmental Factor Updates – to organizational performance appraisals and personnel skill records
- Organizational Process Assets Updates – to historical information, templates, and processes
- Change Requests – to the plan, possibly stemming from staffing changes

Copyright © Mometrix Media. You have been licensed one copy of this document for personal use only. Any other reproduction or redistribution is strictly prohibited. All rights reserved.

Project communications management

Project Communication Management is a significant part of project management. It is an ongoing process of collecting, generating, maintaining, and distributing project information. It provides a vital information conduit between stakeholders. Its main components are Identifying Stakeholders, Planning Communications, Distributing Information, Managing Stakeholder Expectations, and Reporting Performance. Communication is a multi-faceted activity, which can take one or all of the following forms:

- Internal (within the organization) or external
- Formal (memos or reports) or informal (e-mails, discussions)
- Vertical (up and down the organization) or horizontal (among peers)
- Official (newsletters and annual reports) or unofficial (off the record)

Communication skills can include effective listening, questioning to gain understanding, increasing team and/or management knowledge, fact-finding, communicating and managing expectations, persuasion, negotiation, conflict resolution, and summarizing.

Identifying stakeholders
Identifying Stakeholders in terms of Project Communication Management may be more detailed than with other aspects of project management in that it requires also identifying stakeholder needs, expectations, level of influence, involvement and impact in the project. This information is needed to determine what kinds of information needs to be communicated to each of the stakeholders, and possibly how and/or how urgently it needs to be communication. For instance, if a stakeholder is someone who invested in the project expecting a high rate of return, that person would need to know if the project cost were way higher than expected, therefore reducing the expected profit. Stakeholder identification Inputs include:

- Project Charter – identifying stakeholders and other parties to the project
- Procurement Documents – identifying stakeholders and/or suppliers
- Enterprise Environmental Factors – such as organizational structure and industry standards
- Organizational Process Assets – including stakeholder registers and lessons learned

Tools and Techniques include Stakeholder Analysis and Expert Judgment. Stakeholder Analysis involves a detailed identification of all stakeholders. The next step in the process of identifying stakeholders is to categorize them, possibly in a chart, according to their influence, power, involvement, ability to impact the project, etc. Once this information is obtained, their respective communication requirements will be easier to ascertain. The Expert Judgment needed for

Copyright © Mometrix Media. You have been licensed one copy of this document for personal use only. Any other reproduction or redistribution is strictly prohibited. All rights reserved.

identifying stakeholders encompasses organization and project management, key stakeholders, subject matter experts, industry groups, and professional associations. Outputs of identifying stakeholders include:

- Stakeholder Register – including their name, role in the organization or project, and contact information
- Assessment Information – including expectations, potential influence, and most important phases of the project
- Stakeholder Classification – internal/external, supporter/neutral/resistor, etc.
- Stakeholder Management Strategy – most effective communication approach to increase stakeholder support and minimize negativity

Planning communications

Planning Communications is a process that is often done early in the life of a project, and entails developing a clear strategy for effectively communicating necessary information, but only that which is necessary, in a timely and responsible manner. It means developing a plan for distributing information as needed, and not distributing information to the wrong parties or before it has been verified, etc. Improper communication can be just as damaging to a project and its stakeholders as withholding pertinent information. Its Inputs include:

- Stakeholder Register
- Stakeholder Management Strategy
- Enterprise Environmental Factors – for communications, all enterprise environmental factors are potential input
- Organizational Process Assets – particularly lessons learned and other historical information

Tools and Techniques include:

- Communication Requirements Analysis – a systematic study of organizational structure, hierarchical department structures, internal, external and stakeholder communication needs—presenting a clear picture of who needs to know what, and how best to communicate the information.
- Communication Technology – choice of technology can be impacted by urgency of need for the information, duration of the project, proximity of the interested parties, and available staffing. Sending an e-mail to someone who sits next to you would be inefficient, as would personally phoning each of 25 people who could receive a group e-mail.
- Communication Models – including the basic model of encoding (into a language understood by others), message and feedback, medium (method), and decode (translating back into meaningful ideas)
- Communication Methods – such as interactive (between two people), push (sending out to people with no immediate feedback), and pull (recipients

Copyright © Mometrix Media. You have been licensed one copy of this document for personal use only.
Any other reproduction or redistribution is strictly prohibited. All rights reserved.

actively seeking the information through a website, for instance).

Outputs include a Communication Management Plan and Project Document Updates. A Communication Management Plan encompasses:

- Stakeholder communication requirements
- How the information is to be communicated – including language, format, content, level of detail, method (e-mail, phone, etc.)
- Time frames and frequency for communicating
- Specific persons who are responsible for authorizing, for communicating, and for receiving information
- Reasons for the communication
- Common terminology glossary, and information flow charts
- Clear process for escalating issue communication – such as from lower management to upper management if an issue is not resolved
- Communication time and budget allocations
- Communication constraints
- Methods for updating the communication management plan
- Project Document Updates refer to schedule, stakeholder register or stakeholder management strategy.

Distributing information

Distributing Information refers to communicating with stakeholders according to the Communications Management Plan, but also may include unexpected communication that might fall outside of the Plan. It includes various models of sender-receiver, meeting management, presentation using visual aids and body language, facilitation, writing, or a choice of available media. Its Inputs include:

- Project Management Plan
- Performance Reports – pivotal documents indicating project status, changes, estimates, forecasting, etc.
- Organizational Process Assets – policies, procedures, templates, lessons learned

Tools and Techniques include communication methods such as meetings or e-mails, also information distribution tools such as websites, hard-copy memos, videoconferencing, etc. Outputs include organizational process assets updates, such as stakeholder notifications, project records, reports, presentations; stakeholder feedback, lessons learned documentation.

Managing Stakeholder Expectations
Managing Stakeholder Expectations involves clear two-way communication, understanding stakeholder expectations, and addressing and resolving issues as they arise.

Its Inputs include:

- Stakeholder Register
- Stakeholder Management Strategy

Copyright © Mometrix Media. You have been licensed one copy of this document for personal use only. Any other reproduction or redistribution is strictly prohibited. All rights reserved.

- Project Management Plan
- Issue Log – to document and monitor resolution of issues in order to maintain clear communication and a health working relationship with stakeholders. Change Log
- Organizational Process Assets – including communication requirements, issue management procedures, change control procedures, and historical information.

Its Tools and Techniques include communication methods, interpersonal skills such as active listening, conflict resolution and trust building; also management skills related to presentation, writing, negotiation, public speaking, etc.

Outputs include:
- Organizational Process Assets – including causes of issues, reasons behind actions, and lessons learned
- Change Requests
- Project Management Plan Updates
- Project Document Updates – including stakeholder management strategy, stakeholder register, and issue log

Reporting Performance

Reporting Performance in terms of Project Communication Management relates to communicating performance status information including progress reports and forecasts. It involves the collection, analysis and reporting of baseline versus actual data. It incorporates analysis and reporting, respectively, of past performance, current status, work completed and to be completed, summary of changes, and other relevant information. Its Inputs include:
- Project Management Plan – including cost, scope and cost baselines
- Work Performance Information – including status of deliverables, schedule, and costs incurred
- Work Performance Measurements – planned versus actual for schedule, cost and technical
- Budget Forecasts
- Organizational Process Assets – such as report templates, policies and procedures regarding measurement indicators, variance limits

Tools and Techniques include:
- Variance Analysis - which assesses possible causes for variances between the baseline and actual.
- Forecasting Methods – including time series methods using historical data, causal/econometric methods looking at external factors such as weather, judgmental or intuitive methods, etc.
- Communication Methods – usual method of communication for reporting performance is a push method.

Outputs include:

Copyright © Mometrix Media. You have been licensed one copy of this document for personal use only. Any other reproduction or redistribution is strictly prohibited. All rights reserved.

- Performance Reports – including analysis, status reports, work completed and to be completed, summary of changes, results of variance analysis, forecasts, etc.
- Organizational Process Assets Updates – included report formats, lessons learned documentation regarding cause and effect, etc.
- Change Requests – recommending corrective or preventive action

Project risk management

Project Risk Management is a matter of identifying and preparing for both known risks and unexpected risks. By definition, a risk is an uncertain event or condition, such as a chocolate supplier's machine breaking down. Known risks are those that can be somewhat expected, such as shipping times during hurricane season. Risks can have various causes, such as requirements or conditions that can affect a project's schedule, scope, cost or quality. Risk management is a combination of developing a contingency plan for known risks and a strategy for managing unexpected risks. It includes the following components:
- Planning Risk Management
- Identifying Risks
- Performing Qualitative Risk Analysis
- Performing Quantitative Risk Analysis
- Plan Risk Responses
- Monitoring and Controlling Risks

Planning risk management
Planning Risk Management is a proactive process that begins on project commencement and should be in place shortly thereafter. It includes strategies for managing risk in an effective and efficient manner, so that actions taken are sufficient but not over-reactive. Appropriate resources should be allocated for risk management. Its Inputs include the Project Scope Statement, Cost Management Plan, Schedule Management Plan, Communications Management Plan, Enterprise Environmental Factors, and Organizational Process Assets such as risk categories, common definitions of terms and concepts, risk statement formats and appropriate templates, roles and responsibilities, authority levels, lessons learned and stakeholder registers. The primary Tools and Techniques are planning meetings and analysis. Planning meetings are usually attended by management and stakeholders who are responsible for responding to risk, and the agenda is developing and defining risk management procedures.

The primary Output is a Risk Management Plan which includes:
- Methodology – approaches, tools and data sources
- Clearly Defined Roles and Responsibilities – for responding to and managing risk
- Budgeting and Timing Parameters
- Risk Categories – providing a systematic structure for identifying risks
- Definitions of Risk Probability and Impact – how likely is a risk to

Copyright © Mometrix Media. You have been licensed one copy of this document for personal use only. Any other reproduction or redistribution is strictly prohibited. All rights reserved.

occur, and what could the potential impact be
- Probability and Impact Matrix – prioritized according to likelihood and impact
- Revised Stakeholder Tolerances
- Reporting Formats – delineating how risk management processes will be documented, analyzed and communicated
- Tracking.

Identifying Risks

Identifying Risks refers to recognizing, documenting and communicating which risks may affect the project. Risk identification may be done by managers, stakeholders, risk management experts, other members of the project team, or external users, or subject matter experts.

Inputs include the Risk Management Plan, Activity Cost Estimates, Activity Duration Estimates, Scope Baseline, Stakeholder Register; Cost, Schedule and Quality Management Plans; Project Documents such as assumptions logs, work performance reports, earned value reports, network diagrams, etc.; Enterprise Environmental Factors such as commercial databases, academic and industry studies, published checklists, benchmarking, risk attitudes, and Organizational Process Assets such as project data files, organizational and project process controls, risk statement templates, and lessons learned. The primary Output is a Risk Register, which includes lists of identified risks and lists of potential responses. Tools and Techniques include:

- Careful and structured Documentation Reviews
- Information Gathering Techniques – such as brainstorming, the Delphi technique, interviewing and root cause analysis.
- Checklist Analysis – primarily based on historical information
- Assumptions Analysis – assesses the validity of project assumptions
- Diagramming Techniques

Qualitative risk analysis

Qualitative Risk Analysis refers to assessing the likelihood of risk and its potential impact, to determine the need for response. Some of the factors involved in risk analysis are determining an organization's or project's risk tolerance, or how vulnerable its scope, schedule, cost and quality are to risk. Also involved is the projected time frame for responding to a risk. Incorporated in qualitative risk analysis are clearly established definitions of risk likelihood and impact. Other factors include risk attitudes of the management team, and recognition of relevant bias. Its Inputs include the Risk Register, Risk Management Plan, Project Scope Statement, and Organizational Process Assets such as historical information, studies of similar projects, and risk databases.

Tools and Techniques include:
- Risk Probability and Impact Assessment – including the level

Copyright © Mometrix Media. You have been licensed one copy of this document for personal use only. Any other reproduction or redistribution is strictly prohibited. All rights reserved.

of probability and its impact on project components

- Probability and Impact Matrix – resulting in a risk rating, following predetermined rules
- Risk Data Quality Assessment – analyzing the credibility of the data
- Risk Categorization
- Risk Urgency Assessment – using indicators of priority such closeness to project completion, time to respond, etc.
- Expert Judgment – risk management expertise

The primary Output is a Risk Register Update which incorporates a ranking list of risks, risks grouped by categories, causes of risk or project areas needing attention, risks identified as needing immediate attention or future analysis, low priority risks, and risk trends.

Quantitative risk analysis

Quantitative Risk Analysis assigns numerical ratings to risk situations and factors. It is usually applied to high-priority risks that have been identified during the qualitative risk analysis. Its Inputs include the Risk Register, Risk Management Plan, Cost and Schedule Management Plans, and Organizational Process Assets such as information on prior or similar projects, also risk databases. Its primary Output is a Risk Register Update which includes:

- Probabilistic analysis – a numerical distribution analysis of project impact and confidence

levels often including cost contingencies

- Probability of achieving cost and time objectives – expressed as a percentage, and possibly graphically
- Prioritized list of quantified risks – those that pose the greatest risk, or present the largest opportunity to the project
- Trends in quantitative risk analysis – which may affect future risk responses.

Plan risk responses

Plan Risk Responses refers to responding to risks by their priority as determined during the qualitative and quantitative analyses. It involves inserting the resources and activities needed to respond to the risk(s) by either lessening negative impacts or enhancing positive impacts. It is not done in isolation, but rather must be agreed upon by all parties, and be cost effective and realistic. Because of this, it is best to have several risk response options available before deciding on the best course or action. Risk Response also includes assigning a single person, known as the Risk Response Owner, to be ultimately responsible for each risk response. Its Inputs include the Risk Register and Risk Management Plan.

Its Tools and Techniques are varied, and each is not necessarily applicable to every type of threat. The basic categories of responses include:

- Strategies for Negative Risks or Threats – including avoidance, or

- 42 -

Copyright © Mometrix Media. You have been licensed one copy of this document for personal use only. Any other reproduction or redistribution is strictly prohibited. All rights reserved.

changing the management plan, transferring the risk to another party—usually in the case of financial risk, mitigating or lessening the impact, or it might be necessary to accept the risk and deal with the consequences.

- Strategies for Positive Risks or Opportunities – risks as unexpected events may be positive, and can be beneficial to the project by strategies of exploiting or embracing the unexpected event, also sharing or allocating the resources to another party; enhancing or increasing the positive impact, also accepting.
- Contingent Response Strategies – responding to the occurrence of a certain event or circumstance, as predetermined by the group.
- Expert Judgment.

The Outputs of Plan Risk Reponses include:

- Risk Register Updates – including identified risks, agreed-upon risk strategies and responsibility assignment; triggers, symptoms and warning signs of risks; actions budgets and schedule activities of responses; contingency plans, residual and secondary risks; and contingency reserves
- Risk-Related Contract Decisions – referring to risk transfers, affecting insurance policies, for instance
- Project Management Plan Updates – including cost, schedule,

procurement and human resource management plans; work breakdown structures, schedule and cost performance baselines

- Project Document Updates – including assumptions log updates, and technical documentation updates.

Monitoring and Controlling Risks

Monitoring and Controlling Risks is an ongoing and somewhat cyclical process of implementing risk responses, tracking known risks, monitoring residual risks, and evaluating the effectiveness of the risk response system. It allows project management to determine if their assumptions, analyses, policies and procedures related to risk are still valid.

The Inputs include the Risk Register, Project Management Plan, Performance Reports and Work Performance Information related to deliverables and schedule status, also costs incurred.

The Tools and Techniques include:

- Risk Assessment – identifying new risks and reassessing or closing current risks
- Risk Audits – assessing the effectiveness of risk responses
- Variance and Trend Analysis
- Technical Performance Measurement – compares planned to actual technical accomplishment
- Reserve Analysis
- Status Meetings

Copyright © Mometrix Media. You have been licensed one copy of this document for personal use only. Any other reproduction or redistribution is strictly prohibited. All rights reserved.

Outputs include:

- Risk Register Updates – including outcomes of risk audits and risk reviews
- Organizational Process Assets Updates – to risk management templates, probability and impact matrix, risk breakdown structure, and lessons learned
- Change Requests – including corrective and preventive action
- Project Management Plan Updates
- Project Document Updates

Project procurement management

Project Procurement Management encompasses various aspects of obtaining goods or services from an outside entity. It involves Planning Procurements, Conducting Procurements, Administering Procurements, and Closing Procurements. It will most likely include a legal, binding contract that will need to be reviewed by not only project management but also possibly by legal reviewers within the organization. Although the organization could be either a buyer or seller of these goods or service, most like they would be the buyer in keeping with the duty or task of Project Procurement Management. Because of the nature of contracts, it is quite likely that the buyer will become a customer stakeholder in the seller's provided services or goods. The terms and conditions could become factors, inputs, or constraints in a project.

Planning Procurements

Planning Procurements involves identifying needs for goods or services that cannot be met internally, researching and identifying outside suppliers. Some factors to consider include who should obtain necessary licenses, if the supplier's policies or scheduling constraints can impact the project cost, scope and scheduling, and if the acquisition/contract could pose an added risk, or perhaps give an opportunity for risk transfer. Its Inputs include:

- Project Scope Statement
- Scope Baseline – including scope statement, work breakdown structure and WBS dictionary
- Requirements Documentation
- Teaming Agreements – identifying predetermined buyer and seller roles, scope of work, competition requirements, etc.
- Enterprise Environmental Factors – including marketplace conditions, other goods and services available, other suppliers, typical terms and conditions for like acquisitions, unique local requirements
- Organizational Process Assets – such as formal procurement policies, relevant management systems, list of pre-qualified suppliers
- Also: Risk Register, Risk-Related Contract Decisions, Project Schedule, Activity Cost Estimates, Cost Performance Baseline

Tools and Techniques include:

- Make-or-Buy Analysis – assessing whether would be better to produce a good or service internally or procure externally

- 44 -

Copyright © Mometrix Media. You have been licensed one copy of this document for personal use only. Any other reproduction or redistribution is strictly prohibited. All rights reserved.

- Expert Judgment – legal, business, purchasing and possibly technical expertise
- Contract Types – including firm fixed price (FFP), fixed price incentive fee (FPIF), fixed price with economic adjustment (FP-EPA), cost-reimbursable, cost plus fixed fee (CPFF), cost plus incentive fee (CPIF), cost plus award fee (CPAF), or time and material (T&M).

Outputs include:
- Procurement Management Plan – delineating specifics of procurement such types of contracts, managing multiple suppliers, how to address variables such as time schedules or make-or-buy decisions, etc.
- Procurement Statements of Work (SOW) – isolated description of the exact portion of the project that is to be contracted out, made available to the seller or potential seller.
- Make-or-Buy Decisions
- Procurement Documents – used to solicit proposals from sellers
- Source Selection Criteria – used to evaluate potential sellers in relation to project needs
- Change Requests

Conducting procurements
Conducting Procurement includes obtaining seller responses, choosing a seller, and awarding a contract. Its Inputs include the Project Management Plan, Procurement Documents, Source Selection Criteria, Qualified Seller List, Seller Proposals, and Project Documents including Risk Register and risk-related contract decisions, Make-or-Buy Decision, Teaming Agreements, and Organizational Process Assets such as listings of previously qualified sellers or information on past sellers. Its Tools and Techniques include:
- Bidder Conferences – meetings between the buyer and prospective seller(s)
- Proposal Evaluation Techniques – a formal evaluation review process which may entail weighted criteria
- Independent Estimate – possibly providing a benchmark or comparison figure
- Expert Judgment – usually a review team comprised of individuals with relevant expertise
- Advertising
- Internet Search
- Procurement Negotiations – clarifying the terms of the purchases before a formal contract is drawn up

Outputs of Conducting Procurements include:
- Project Scope Statement
- Selected Sellers
- Contract Award – possibly including statement of work or deliverables, schedule baseline, performance reporting, period of performance, roles and responsibilities, seller's place of

- 45 -

Copyright © Mometrix Media. You have been licensed one copy of this document for personal use only. Any other reproduction or redistribution is strictly prohibited. All rights reserved.

performance, pricing and payment terms, place of delivery, warranty, product support, liability limitation, penalties and incentives, insurance, change request and termination specifics.

- Resource Calendars
- Change Requests
- Project Management Plan Updates – possibly affecting cost, scope and schedule baselines, also procurement management plan
- Project Document Update – including requirements documentation and risk register

Administering Procurements

Administering Procurements is the process of overseeing and managing the awarded contract and the contractual relation-ship. It may be handled outside of the project team. It includes: Directing and Managing Project Execution, Reporting Performance, Performing Quality Control, Performing Integrated Change Control, and Monitoring and Controlling Risks.

Inputs include Procurement Documents, Project Management Plan, Contract, Seller Performance Reports, Approved Change Requests, and Work/Performance Information.

Tools and Techniques include:
- Contract Change Control System – defines how a procurement can be modified
- Procurement Performance Reviews – assessing scope,

quality, cost and schedule compared to contract
- Inspections and Audits
- Performance Reporting – information provided to management. Payment Systems – payment should be contingent on satisfactory work
- Claims Administration – claims are documented, processed, monitored and managed throughout the contract life cycle
- Records Management System

Outputs include:
- Procurement Documentation – a comprehensive portfolio of documents related to the procurement contract
- Organizational Process Assets Updates – including correspondence regarding contract terms, payment schedules and requests, and seller performance documentation
- Change Requests. Project Management Plan Updates – including Procurement Management Plan and baseline schedule.

Closing procurements

Closing Procurements relates to closing the contract or agreement, including finalizing claims and records, and verification that work and deliverables were satisfactory. However, procurement closing may also occur in the case of early termination of contract, either mutually agreed upon or upon the default of one of the parties. Inputs for Closing

- 46 -

Copyright © Mometrix Media. You have been licensed one copy of this document for personal use only. Any other reproduction or redistribution is strictly prohibited. All rights reserved.

Procurements include the Project Management Plan and Procurement Documentation.

Its Tools and Techniques include:
- Procurement Audit – comprehensive from the planning through the administration processes, to identify successes and failures for future procurement endeavors
- Negotiated Settlements – handled by the buyer and seller unless they cannot agree, in which case an outside mediator is employed.
- Records Management System

Outputs include Closed Procurements, and Organizational Process Assets Updates including procurement file, deliverable acceptance, and lessons learned documentation.

Decision Criteria

It is essential that all solutions be evaluated against the same set of criteria:
- Business Process Impact – Describe how the potential solution will impact the current business processes and what degree of organizational change and stakeholder resistance is anticipated.
- Technical Feasibility - Describe any special considerations such as technical experience required for project team members. Also, describe the level of technical complexity associated with the solution.
- Maturity of Solution - Describe the level of technical maturity for the potential solution. The description should address how technically proven the potential solution is, for example: Is the solution a recent innovation? Has it fully matured? Is it nearing obsolescence? Are service and expertise readily available to support the potential technical solution?
- Resources Estimate – Estimate all the resources required to implement the solution. Resources include personnel, facilities, customer support, equipment, and any other resources needed to implement the solution.
- Constraints Impact – Describe how well the solution fits within the identified constraints. Specifically address any time or schedule constraints.

Project information

The following is the basic information that identifies the project:
- General Information – Basic information that identifies the project.
- Project Title – The proper name used to identify this project.
- Project Working Title – The working name or acronym used to identify the project. If an acronym is used, define the specific meaning of each letter.

Copyright © Mometrix Media. You have been licensed one copy of this document for personal use only. Any other reproduction or redistribution is strictly prohibited. All rights reserved.

- Prepared by – The person(s) preparing this document.
- Date Prepared – The date this document is initially prepared

Risk analysis summary

The following are the basics of Risk analysis summary:
- Risk Number - Assign a Risk Number to each risk.
- Risk Name - Provide a Risk Name or title for the risk.
- Probability of Occurrence – Identify, as a percentage, the likelihood that the risk event will occur.
- Impact Level - Provide a value (between 1 and 5) for the impact the risk will have on the project. A value of one (1) is the least impact and a value of five (5) is the highest impact.
- Impact Description - Describe the impact of the risk is if it occurs.
- Time Frame - Estimate the actual date or timeframe in which the risk is most likely to occur. Timeframes are provided in fiscal years and quarters – if known.

Project charter and project scope

The Project Charter documents the project scope. Project Scope defines all of the products and services delivered by a project, and identify the limits of the project. In other words, the scope establishes the boundaries of a project. The Project Scope addresses the who, what, where, when, and why of a project.

The Project Charter explicitly identifies the project manager and gives him the authority to plan, execute, and control the project. The Project Charter establishes a relationship between the project manager and senior management to ensure support mechanisms exist to resolve issues outside the authority of the project manager. The Project Charter will indicate the resources that the project sponsor and management will commit to the project. This includes people, facilities, equipment, and funding.

WBS

A Work Breakdown Structure (WBS) requires that a parent-child (hierarchical) relationship be established. To achieve the parent-child relationship, a simple coding scheme will be used to assign a numerical identification number to each element. Responsible Person or Group – Assign responsibility for the WBS Element to a person or group on or associated with the project team. Further decomposition of the WBS Element and cost estimation may be part of the assigned responsibility. The information in this column is used in developing the organizational breakdown structure. Estimated (E) or Actual (A) Cost – Provide an estimated or actual cost, if known, for the completion of the WBS Element. This column is completed after the decomposition to the lowest task level is complete. Begin at the smallest element and roll up cost to the larger elements. This provides a foundation for the budget (expenditures) plan.

- 48 -

Copyright © Mometrix Media. You have been licensed one copy of this document for personal use only. Any other reproduction or redistribution is strictly prohibited. All rights reserved.

Project Phase – Most complex projects are executed in phases. Identify the phase in which the WBS Element will occur. The phase must be synchronized with the project schedule.

Analysis of change request

The change request originator or other designated individual will provide detailed information on the impact the change will have on the project:

- Impact on Change or Configuration Item – Describe the impact on change and configuration control items.
- Impact on Project Budget - Detail the impact of implementing the change to the Project Budget.
- Impact on Project Schedule – Detail the impact of implementing the change to the Project Schedule.
- Impact on other Project Resources – Detail the impact of implementing the change to the other project resources.

CV and SV

The relationship between CV and SV is described below:

- If CV is positive and SV is negative, either the task has not started or it has started and not enough resources have been applied.
- If CV is negative and SV is negative, the costs are overrun and the schedule is slipping.

- If CV is negative and SV is positive, this indicates that money was spent to crash the schedule.
- If CV is positive and SV is positive, the project is under budget and ahead of schedule.

CPIF and FPIF contracts

CPIF-Cost Plus Incentive Fee, Seller is paid for allowable performance costs along with a predetermined fee and an incentive bonus, Long performance period with hardware & development test requirements; compute incentive based on savings; Original price = 10,000, fee = 1,000, 80/20 share; final price 8,000 buyer pays 8,000+1,000+400 (20% of 2,000 savings).

FPIF-Fixed Price Incentive Fee, The most complex type of contract, which is composed of a target cost, target profit, target price, ceiling price, and share ratio, usually used when contracts are for substantial sum and involve a long production time. This enables the seller to develop production efficiency during the performance of the contract. Target cost 100,000, target price 110,000, target profit 10,000, ceiling price 12,000, share ratio 70/30; if cost above 120,000 no profit.

CPPC and CPFF contracts

CPPC-Cost Plus Percentage of Costs, Buyer assumes risk, provides for reimbursement to the contractor for allowable costs due to contract performance. Additionally, the contractor

Copyright © Mometrix Media. You have been licensed one copy of this document for personal use only. Any other reproduction or redistribution is strictly prohibited. All rights reserved.

receives an agreed-upon percentage of the estimated costs as a profit. Although prohibited in federal government, used in private, particularly construction industry.

CPFF-Cost Plus Fixed Fee, Buyer high risk; Seller moderate risk, Provides that the seller be reimbursed for allowable costs for performing the contract, and in addition the seller receives a profit a fixed fee payment usually based on a % of estimated costs, for difficult and long research projects.

Deming's 14 Points

Deming 14 Points are:
- Create constant message
- Commitment to continuously improve quality
- Focus on prevention
- Do not award contracts to lowest
- Improve constantly and forever
- Quality training
- Supervision coach and mentor
- Drive out fear
- Eliminate barriers
- Eliminate slogans
- Eliminate management by objectives
- Remove barriers to pride of workmanship
- Institute education & self improvement
- Create an organization to support 1-13

FFP and T&M contracts

FFP-Firm Fixed Price, It is an agreement where the contractor agrees to furnish supplies or services at a specified price that is not subject to adjustment because of performance costs. It is best suited when reasonably definite production specifications are available and costs are relatively certain. Lump sum - used most often; Seller has most risk.

T&M-Time and Materials, Hybrid type of contractual arrangement that contains aspects of both cost-reimbursable and fixed-price-type arrangement. Based upon performing a prescribed amount of work, previously agreed upon by both the seller and buyer, where the seller is paid for amount of time it takes to accomplish the work. The seller also provides, but is reimbursed, for the materials to complete the work.

Schedule variance

Comparing the value of work performed with the value of work scheduled determines Schedule Variance (SV). SV is a subjective indicator. It does not reveal the critical path. SV is an aggregate dollarized value of events ahead or behind schedule.

Commercial Projects
SV = P - SW

Government Projects
SV = BCWP - BCWS

A positive schedule variance is an indication that in-process work is ahead of schedule. A negative schedule variance

- 50 -

Copyright © Mometrix Media. You have been licensed one copy of this document for personal use only. Any other reproduction or redistribution is strictly prohibited. All rights reserved.

indicates that the in-process work is behind schedule.

80/20 rule

The 80/20 Rule means that in anything a few (20 percent) are vital and many (80 percent) are trivial. In Pareto's case it meant 20 percent of the people owned 80 percent of the wealth. In Juran's initial work he identified 20 percent of the defects causing 80 percent of the problems. Project Managers know that 20 percent of the work (the first 10 percent and the last 10 percent) consumes 80 percent of your time and resources. You can apply the 80/20 Rule to almost anything, from the science of management to the physical world.

You know 20 percent of your stock takes up 80 percent of your warehouse space and that 80 percent of your stock comes from 20 percent of your suppliers. Also 80 percent of your sales will come from 20 percent of your sales staff. 20 percent of your staff will cause 80 percent of your problems, but another 20 percent of your staff will provide 80 percent of your production. It works both ways.

Schedule performance index

The ratio of work accomplished versus work planned, for a specified period of time, defines the Schedule Performance Index (SPI). The SPI is an efficiency rating for work accomplishment. The SPI compares work accomplished to what should have been accomplished.

Commercial Projects
$$SPI = P/SW$$

Government Projects
$$SPI = BCWP/BCWS$$

This formula produces a SPI that is referred to as SPIe. The e is an efficiency designation. The inverse of the formula, $SW/P = SPIp$. The p is a performance designation. The analyst should designate which SPI is being used in the Schedule Variance discussion. The analyst needs to keep in mind and be aware that a SPI of 100% indicates an on schedule condition. However, this performance indication may not necessarily provide the true status of the work accomplished, since some work may have been performed out of sequence or ahead of schedule. The Task Plan and program schedules shall be used in conjunction with the SPI to provide valid Work In Process (WIP) status information.

Cost variance

Comparing the value of work performed with the actual cost of work performed determines Cost Variance (CV). CV is an objective indicator. CV is a dollarized value of what was accomplished for the resources expended. Arithmetically, this is expressed as:
Commercial Projects
$$CV = P - A$$

Government Projects
$$CV = BCWP - ACWP$$

Copyright © Mometrix Media. You have been licensed one copy of this document for personal use only. Any other reproduction or redistribution is strictly prohibited. All rights reserved.

A positive cost variance indicates that work was accomplished for less resource expenditure than planned. A negative cost variance indicates that work accomplished cost more than planned resource value.

Cost performance index

The Cost Performance Index (CPI) is defined as the ratio work accomplished versus work cost incurred for a specified period of time. The CPI is an efficiency rating for work accomplished for resources expended.

Commercial Projects
$CPI = P/A$

Government Projects
$CPI = BCWP/ACWP$

This formula produces a CPI that is referred to as CPIe. The e is an efficiency designation. The inverse of the formula, $A/P = CPIp$. The p is a performance designation. The analysis required to designate which CPI is being used in the Cost Variance discussion.

Variance at completion

Comparing the Budget at Completion (BAC) with the latest Estimate of Completion (EAC) determines the Variance at Completion (VAC). The VAC formula is arithmetically expressed as:

Commercial Projects
$VAC = BAC - EAC$

Government Projects
$VAC = BAC - EAC$

Affinity diagram and benchmarking

And Affinity Diagram is a tool used to organize ideas, usually generated through brainstorming, into groups of related thoughts. The emphasis is on a pre-rational, gut-fell sort of grouping, often done by the members of the group with little or no talking. It is also known as the KJ method after its creator, Kawakita Jiro.

Benchmarking is a technique that involves comparing one's own processes to excellent examples of similar processes in other organizations or departments. Through benchmarking, rapid learning can occur, and processes can undergo dramatic improvements.

Juran's steps for quality planning

Juran even went so far as to provide us with a roadmap for quality planning. This roadmap consisted of 10 steps, with one overriding principle. The overall principle requires us to apply measurements to each step. The steps are:
- Customers
- Discover Customers' Needs
- Translate the Customers' Needs into our Language
- Establish Units of Measure
- Establish Measurement
- Develop Product
- Optimize Product Design
- Develop the Process

Copyright © Mometrix Media. You have been licensed one copy of this document for personal use only. Any other reproduction or redistribution is strictly prohibited. All rights reserved.

- Optimize: Prove the Process Capability
- Transfer to Operations

Control chart and control limit

A control chart is a chart that indicates upper and lower statistical control limits, and an average line, for samples or subgroups of a given process. If all points on the control chart are within the limits, variation may be ascribed to common causes and the process is deemed to be "in control." If points fall outside the limits, it is an indication that special causes of variation are occurring, and the process is said to be "out of control."

A control limit is a statistically determined line on a control chart used to analyze variation within a process. If variation exceeds the control limits, then the process is being affected by special causes and is said to be "out of control." A control limit is not the same as a specification limit.

Chart types

Cause & Effect diagram
A tool used to analyze all factors (causes) that contribute to a given situation or occurrence (effect) by breaking down main causes into smaller and smaller sub-causes. It is also known as the Ishikawa or the fishbone diagram.

Count chart (c chart)
An attributes data control chart that evaluates process stability by charting the

counts of occurrences of a given event in successive samples.

Count-per-unit chart (u chart)
A control chart that evaluates process stability by charting the number of occurrences of a given event per unit sampled, in a series of samples.

Mean, median and mode

Mean is the average of a group of measurement values. Mean is determined by dividing the sum of the values by the number of values in the group.

Median is the middle of a group of measurement values when arranged in numerical order. For example, in the group (32, 45, 78, 79, 101), 78 is the median. If the group contains an even number of values, the median is the average of the two middle values.

Mode is the most frequently occurring value in a group of measurements.

Decision matrix

Decision Matrix is a tool used to evaluate problems, solutions, or ideas. The possibilities are listed down the left-hand side of the matrix and relevant criteria are listed across the top. Each possibility is then rated on a numeric scale of importance or effectiveness (e.g. on a scale of 1 to 10) for each criterion, and each rating is recorded in the appropriate box. When all ratings are complete, the scores for each possibility are added to determine which has the highest overall

Copyright © Mometrix Media. You have been licensed one copy of this document for personal use only. Any other reproduction or redistribution is strictly prohibited. All rights reserved.

rating and thus deserves the greatest attention.

5 project phases

The 5 Project Phases can be remembered using the IPECC Acronym:
- Initiation
- Planning
- Execution
- Control
- Closing

PDCA cycle

The Plan-Do-Check-Act (PDCA) cycle is a four-step improvement process originally conceived of by Walter A. Shewhart. The first step involves planning for the necessary improvement; the second step is the implementation of the plan; the third step is to check the results of the plan; the last step is to act upon the results of the plan. It is also known as the Shewhart cycle, the Deming cycle, and the PDCA cycle.

Project triage

An experienced Project Manager should perform a Project Triage. In some cases it may be more effective to secure a Project Manager from outside the Performing Organization, who is less likely to be influenced by organizational politics, history, or other factors. Inside knowledge can sometimes limit the effectiveness of a triage by prejudicially eliminating ideas without proper consideration. While having the triage per-formed by another Project Manager

within the organization who has not previously been involved in the project may be more objective, it still may be difficult for anyone from within the organization to evaluate the work of a peer. In general, the less background related to the project and the Performing Organization the Project Manager has before taking on the project triage, the more likely it is that the effort will produce objective and effective results. However, the reality is that a Project Manager often triages his or her own project.

Gantt chart

A Gantt chart is a horizontal bar chart developed as a production control tool in 1917 by Henry L. Gantt, an American engineer and social scientist. Frequently used in project management, a Gantt chart provides a graphical illustration of a schedule that helps to plan, coordinate, and track specific tasks in a project. A Gantt chart is constructed with a horizontal axis represent-in the total time span of the project, broken down into increments (for example, days, weeks, or months) and a vertical axis representing the tasks that make up the project (for example, if the project is outfitting your computer with new software, the major tasks involved might be: conduct research, choose software, install software). Horizontal bars of varying lengths represent the sequences, timing, and time span for each task. Using the same example, you would put "conduct research" at the top of the vertical axis and draw a bar on the graph that

- 54 -

Copyright © Mometrix Media. You have been licensed one copy of this document for personal use only. Any other reproduction or redistribution is strictly prohibited. All rights reserved.

represents the amount of time you expect to spend on the research, and then enter the other tasks below the first one and representative bars at the points in time when you expect to undertake them. The bar spans may overlap, as, for example, you may conduct research and choose software during the same time span. As the project progresses, secondary bars, arrowheads, or darkened bars may be added to indicate completed tasks, or the portions of tasks that have been completed. A vertical line is used to represent the report date.

Project planning

The purpose of Project Planning is to define the exact parameters of a project and ensure that all the pre-requisites for Project Execution and Control are in place. Project Planning builds upon the work performed during Project Initiation. The project definition and scope are validated with appropriate Stakeholders, starting with the Project Sponsor and Customer Decision-Makers. Project Scope, Schedule and Budget are refined and confirmed, and risk assessment activities advance to the mitigation stage.

Additional Project Team members are brought on board and familiarized with the project objectives and environment, and additional resources are ready to be brought in following the finalized staff and material acquisition plans.

Project Planning is an opportunity to identify and resolve any remaining issues and answer outstanding questions that may undermine the goals of the project or threaten its success. It is an opportunity to plan and prepare, as opposed to react and catch up.

Project closeout

The purpose of Project Closeout is to assess the project and derive any lessons learned and best practices to be applied to future projects.

Project Closeout begins with a Post-Implementation Review. The review may start with a survey designed to solicit feedback on the project from the Project Team, Customers, Consumers and other stakeholders. Once feedback has been collected and evaluated, an assessment meeting is conducted to derive best practices and formulate lessons learned to inform future efforts. Ideally, the best practices and lessons learned should be stored in a centralized organizational repository, facilitating access and retrieval by managers of future projects.

Project Closeout ends with administrative closeout Ð providing feedback on Project Team members, updating the skills inventory, capturing key project metrics, and filing all pertinent project materials into the project repository.

Performance measures

Performance Measures should identify the population to be measured, the method of the measurement, and the data source and time period for the

Copyright © Mometrix Media. You have been licensed one copy of this document for personal use only. Any other reproduction or redistribution is strictly prohibited. All rights reserved.

measurement. Each measure should also be:

- Objective
- Easy to understand
- Controllable by minimizing outside influences
- Timely
- Accurate
- Cost-effective
- Useful
- Motivating
- Trackable

Performance Measures are quantitative or qualitative ways to characterize and define performance. They provide a tool for organizations to manage progress towards achieving predetermined goals, defining key indicators of organizational performance and Customer satisfaction.

Project execution and control

The purpose of Project Execution and Control is to develop the product or service that the project was commissioned to deliver. Typically, this is the longest phase of the project management lifecycle, where most resources are applied.

Project Execution and Control utilizes all the plans, schedules, procedures and templates that were prepared and anticipated during prior phases. Unanticipated events and situations will inevitably be encountered, and the Project Manager and Project

The conclusion of the phase arrives when the product of the project is fully developed, tested, accepted, implemented and transitioned to the Performing Organization.

Accurate records need to be kept throughout this phase. They serve as input to the final phase, Project Closeout.

Turnkey procurement

A turnkey procurement involves securing a complete vendor-supplied solution that is provided to the Customer "ready to operate" (just turn the key). The contracted vendor acquires all the necessary parts, products and services, and all required labor to construct and install the turnkey solution. This type of procurement requires the contractor to perform the day-to-day management of the Project Team and project processes, while the Project Manager focuses on contractor performance and management of the product transition to the Performing Organization.

In a turnkey procurement, the purchaser generally takes ownership of all products purchased, either at time of purchase or at time of transition, depending on the contract terms.

While turnkey procurements are a possible option, it is more likely that the Project Manager will choose to procure several products and services, and to manage the resulting contracts.

Balanced scorecard

Copyright © Mometrix Media. You have been licensed one copy of this document for personal use only. Any other reproduction or redistribution is strictly prohibited. All rights reserved.

The balanced scorecard is a measurement framework that integrates multiple perspectives. The balanced scorecard integrates four sets of measurements, complementing traditional financial measures with those driving future performance. An organization using this framework is encouraged to develop metrics that facilitate collection and analysis of information from the following perspectives:

- Financial
- Customer
- Learning and Growth
- Internal Business Processes

Implementation of a balanced scorecard presents an opportunity for a Performing Organization to look at its existing programs, services, and processes. Are the right services being provided to the Customers? (Are we doing the right things?) Are the processes implemented now the most efficient and cost effective?

Active listening techniques and questioning techniques

Active listening techniques include seeking understanding through asking for clarification of the message, paraphrasing to make sure you have understood the message, encouraging dialogue through empathic remarks, and refraining from interrupting and making judgmental remarks.

Examples of questioning techniques are using open-ended questions that call for more than a "yes" or "no" answer, using follow-up questions to obtain additional information, and avoiding leading questions that put the respondent under pressure to respond in a certain way.

Trust between project stakeholders and project manager

Project Stakeholders must trust the Project Manager in order for the Project Manager to be an effective leader. Trust is developed over time, and is most easily inspired when the Project Manager exhibits a willingness and ability to:

- Share information.Personal feelings.
- Listen to and understand others' perspectives.
- Admit mistakes
- Encourage others.
- Confront others
- Keep promises.
- Be credible and sincere
- Be responsible and accountable for actions

Important terms

Acquisition - Obtaining supplies or services by and for the use of an organization through a purchase or lease.
Active Listening - Paying close attention to what is said, asking the other party to describe carefully and clearly what is meant, and requesting that ideas be repeated to clarify any ambiguity or uncertainty.
Activity - Element of work that is required by the project, uses resources, and takes time to complete. Activities have expected durations, costs, and resources

Copyright © Mometrix Media. You have been licensed one copy of this document for personal use only. Any other reproduction or redistribution is strictly prohibited. All rights reserved.

requirements and may be subdivided into tasks.

Acceptance - To agree with or approve a deliverable.

Acceptance Criteria - Requirements that a project or system must demonstrably meet before customers acceptance delivery.

Accounting Period - Set period of time, usually one month, in which project costs and revenues are posted for information and analysis.

Actual Cost (AC) - Total costs incurred that must relate to whatever cost was budgeted within the planned value and earned value (which can sometimes be direct labor hours alone, direct costs alone, or all costs including indirect costs) in accomplishing work during a given time period.

Actual Cost Of Work Performance (ACWP) - Total costs (direct and indirect) incurred in accomplishing work during a given time period.

Actual Finish date (AF) - The point in time that work actually ended on an activity. (Note: In some application areas, the activity is considered "finished" when work is "substantially complete.")

Activity Definition - Identification of specific activities that must be performed to produce the project deliverables. Also called activity description.

Activity Description (AD) - A short phrase or label used in a project network diagram. The activity description normally describes the scope of work of the activity.

Activity Duration Estimating - Estimating the number of work periods needed to complete individual activities.

Affected Groups - The groups who will either be expected to support the project to some degree or whose work, products, or services will be utilized in support of the project or affected by the project outcomes.

Alternatives - The various options available.

Alternatives Analysis - Process of breaking down a complex situation to generate different solutions and approaches and evaluate the impact of trade-offs to attain objectives.

Actual Start date (AS) - The point in time that work actually started on an activity.

Administrative Closure - Activities associated with generating, gathering, and disseminating information to formalize acceptance of the product or service of the project by the sponsor, client, or customer for a specific project phase or at project completion.

Administrative Expense - Expense that cannot be easily identified with a specific function or project but contributes in some way to the project or general business operations.

Approach - Overall method by which project objectives will be realized, including methodologies, life cycles, responsibilities, and other associated strategies, tactics, practices, and procedures.

Arrow Diagramming Method (ADM) - Network diagramming technique in which activities are represented by arrows. The tail of the arrow represents the start of the activity; the head of the arrow represents the finish of the activity. The length of the arrow does not represent the expected duration of the

Copyright © Mometrix Media. You have been licensed one copy of this document for personal use only. Any other reproduction or redistribution is strictly prohibited. All rights reserved.

activity. Activities are connected at points called nodes (usually drawn as circles) to illustrate the sequence in which activities are expected to be performed. Also called activity-on-arrow.

Assumption - Factor that is considered to be true, real, or certain and is often used as a basis for decision-making.

American National Standards Institute (ANSI) - Voluntary organization that helps set standards and also represents the United States in the International Standards Organization (ISO).

Analogous Estimating - Using actual or historical data of a similar activity or project as the basis for the estimate. Analogous estimating is a form of expert judgment.

Analysis - Study and examination of something complex by separating it into a simpler component. Typically, includes discovering the parts of the thing being studied, how they fit together, and why they are arranged in a particular way. Study of variances for cause, impact, corrective action, and results.

Authoritarian Management Style - Management approach in which the project manager tells team members what is expected of them, provides specific guidance on what should be done, makes his or her role within the team understood, schedules work, and directs team members to follow standard rules and regulations.

Authority - Power of influence, either granted to or developed by individuals, that leads to others doing what those individuals direct. Formal conferment of such influence through an instrument such as a project charter.

Authorize - Give final approval; a person who can authorize something is vested with authority to give final endorsement, which requires no further approval.

Attribute - Characteristics or property that is appraised in terms of whether it does or does not exist (for example, heads or tails on a coin) with respect to a given requirement.

Audit - Formal examination of project's accounts or financial situation. Methodical examination of the project, either in whole or in part, usually conducted according to pre-established schedules, to assess overall progress performance.

Audit Trail - Record of documentation describing actions taken, decisions made, and funds expended and earned on a project. Used to reconstruct the project after the fact for lessons learned and other purposes.

Backward Pass - Calculation of late finish and late start dates for uncompleted portions of all network activities. Determined by working backwards through the network logic from the project's end date.

Balanced Matrix - Form of the project organization in which the project manager's authority over project resources is roughly equal to that of the organization's functional managers.

Baseline - Original plan (for a project, work package, or activity), plus or minus any approved changes. May be used with modifier (for example, cost baseline, schedule baseline, performance measurement baseline). Normal plan to which deviations will be compared.

Copyright © Mometrix Media. You have been licensed one copy of this document for personal use only. Any other reproduction or redistribution is strictly prohibited. All rights reserved.

Authorized Work - Efforts that have been approved by higher authority and may or may not be expressed in specific terms.

Autocratic Management Style - Management approach in which the project manager makes all decisions and exercises tight control over the project team. This style is characterized by communications from the project manager downward to the team and not vice versa.

Avoidance - Risk response strategy that eliminates the threat of a specific risk event, usually by eliminating its potential cause. The project management team can never eliminate all risk, but certain risk events often can be eliminated.

Benefit-Cost Analysis - Process of estimating tangible and intangible costs (outlays) and benefits (returns) of various projects alternatives and using financial measures, such as return on investment or payback period, to evaluate the relative desirability of the alternatives.

Bill Of Materials (BOM) - Set of physical elements required to build a project. Hierarchical view of the physical assemblies, subassemblies, and components needed to fabricate a manufacturing product. Descriptive and quantitative list of materials, supplies, parts, and components required to produce a designated complete end item of materials, assembly, or subassembly.

Boilerplate - Standard and essential contract terminology and clauses that are not subject to frequent change. Use of the term can be dangerous because it may lull contract parties into thinking they need not read the clauses, assuming no changes

from previous contracts, or assuming the data are not significant.

Baseline Finish Date - Original planned finish date for a project, work package, or activity, plus or minus any approved changes.

Baseline Start Date - Original planned start date for a project, work package, or activity, plus or minus any approved changes.

Benefit - Gain to be accrued from the successful completion of a project. Benefits are compared to costs to ensure the selection of the most advantageous project or the most effective approach to complete a project.

Budget Estimate - Estimate of the funds needed to obtain project approval, which includes a combination of fixed and unit prices for labor, material, equipment, and other direct and indirect costs.

Budget Update - Change to an approved cost baseline, generally revised only in response to scope changes.

Budgeted Cost Of Work Performed (BCWP) - Sum of approved cost estimates (including any overhead allocation) for activities (or portions of activities) completed during a given period.

Budgeted Cost Of Work Scheduled (BCWS) - Sum of approved cost estimates (including any overhead allocation) for activities (or portions of activities) scheduled to be preformed during a given period.

Bottom-Up Estimating - Cost or budget estimate derived by first estimating the cost of the project's elemental tasks at the lower levels of the WBS and then aggregating those estimates at successively higher levels of the WBS. The

Copyright © Mometrix Media. You have been licensed one copy of this document for personal use only. Any other reproduction or redistribution is strictly prohibited. All rights reserved.

project manager typically includes indirect costs, general and administrative expenses, profit, and any reverses when calculating the total project cost estimate.

Brainstorming - Problem-solving technique that can be used for planning purposes, risk identification, improvement efforts, and other project-related endeavors. Participants are invited to share their ideas in a group setting, where no disapproving verbal or nonverbal behaviors are permitted. The technique is designed to generate a large number of ideas by helping people to think creatively and allowing them to participate fully, without feeling inhibited or criticized by others.

Budget At Completion (BAC) - Sum of approved cost estimates (including any overhead allocation) for all activities in a project.

Business Process Model - Decomposition and graphical depiction a specific business process or functional area within an organization. The model shows how each functional area breaks down into processes; each process breaks down into sub processes; and each sub process breaks down into activities.

Business Process Reengineering - Method to improve organizational performance by evaluating and redesigning business processes.

Champion - Person who spearheads an idea or action and promotes it throughout the organization. Person with significant influence who takes personal responsibility (although usually not for day-to-day management) for the successful completion of a project for the organization.

Bureaucratic Authority - Influence derived from an individual's knowing the organization's rules, regulations, and procedures and the ways to use them to obtain desired results in an expedient and expeditious manner.

Burn Rate - Rate at which funds are expended on a project (for example, total dollars per day or total dollars per week). Usually quoted based on labor hours only, but may include materials as well.

Business Analyst - A person who gathers and/or supplies business requirements for systems development projects, solicits business involvement, and acts as liaison between the business and the project team. They assist in reviewing and providing input to the resulting system design and may assist with system testing and user training.

Business Complexity - This represents the business difficulty or risk associated with a particular business issue or opportunity that is driving a need for change.

Change Control Procedure - Process for initiating changes to the project baseline configuration; analyzing the impact of changes to project cost, schedule, and scope; approving or disapproving changes; and updating project or product specifications and baselines.

Change Management Plan - Premeditated, documented approach to implementing configuration control. Approach used to assimilate a new system or set of procedure in an organization.

Change Request - Request for modification to the terms of the contract or to the description of the product or service to be provided. Formal written

Copyright © Mometrix Media. You have been licensed one copy of this document for personal use only. Any other reproduction or redistribution is strictly prohibited. All rights reserved.

statement asking to make a modification to a deliverable.

Change - Increase or decrease in any project characteristics - time, cost or technical requirements. Deviation from agreed-upon specifications, definition, functionally, or plans; alternate approach to project work accomplishments. Alteration in a contract as permitted by a contract clause.

Change Control - Process of monitoring and dealing with changes to the schedule, cost or scope of a project, or its overall objectives. May be considered a subset of configuration management. Defined process and procedure for change management during the project life cycle.

Change Control Board (CCB) - Formally constituted group of stakeholders responsible for approving or rejecting changes to the project baselines. Also called configuration control board.

Code Review - An iterative process whereby someone other than the developer examines source code and provides feedback regarding development aspects, such as bad constructs, poor structure, ambiguity, commenting, poor algorithms, and adherence to standards and specifications.

Combative Management Style - Management approach in which the project manager displays an eagerness to fight or be disagreeable over any given situation.

Commercial Off The Shelf (COTS) - Item, software application, or service available in the commercial market.

Changes Or Enhancements - Improved, advanced, or sophisticated features.

Charismatic Authority - Influence derived from an individual's personality. People what is asked of them because they like the asker.

Client - Customer, principal, owner, promoter, buyer, or end user of the product or service created by the project.

Closing Processes - Activities associated with formal acceptance of the phase or project and bringing it to an orderly end.

Communication Management Plan - Document that describes the methods for gathering, distributing, and storing various types of information; provides a production schedule showing when each type of information will be produced; details methods for accessing information between scheduled communications; and incorporates procedures for updating and refining the communication plan. Generally, a part of the overall project plan.

Communication Planning - Process used to identify the general or specific information needs of the project stakeholders, the frequency with which the information is presented to them, and the form the communication will take. Also includes general communication such as press releases, articles, and public presentations.

Closing Processes - Activities associated with formal acceptance of the phase or project and bringing it to an orderly end.

Communication - Effective transfer of information from one party to another; exchanging information between individuals through a common system of symbols, signs, or behavior. Communication comprises four elements:

Copyright © Mometrix Media. You have been licensed one copy of this document for personal use only. Any other reproduction or redistribution is strictly prohibited. All rights reserved.

- Communicator or sender of a message,
- Message
- Medium of the message
- Receiver of the message

Communication Channel - Means of communication used to transmit a message. Three communication channel exist in the project environment: Formal-communication within the organization's formal communication structure used to transmit policies, goals, and directives

- Informal-communication outside the organization's formal communication structure; and
- Unofficial-interpersonal communication within the organization's social structure.

Compliance - Adhering to any standards, procedures, or processes established as necessary for operational effectiveness. Meeting all technical, contractual, and price/cost requirements of a request for proposal.

Conceptual Solution - Initial technical approach developed to satisfy project requirements, as they are known early in the project.

Conciliatory Management Style - Management approach in which the project manager is friendly and agreeable and attempts to unite all project parties involved to provide compatible working team.

Conditional Diagramming Method - Diagramming techniques, such as GERT or system dynamic models, that allow non-sequential activities such as loops or conditional branches.

Communication Requirements - Total information needs of project stakeholders. Information necessary for determining project communication requirements includes:

- Project organization and stakeholder responsibility relationships;
- Disciplines, departments, and specialties involved in the project;
- Number of individuals involved in the project and their locations; and
- External information needs (such as communicating with the media)

Competency - Critical skill, or in some cases personality characteristics, required of an individual to complete an activity or project, or otherwise required for a certain position. For example, the ability to think strategically is considered by some to be a critical competency for a person who will be the project manager of a large and complex project.

Completed Activity - Activity with an actual finish date and no remaining duration.

Conflict Resolution - Process if seeking a solution to a problem. Generally, five methods are available:

- Problem solving or confrontation, where two parties work together towards a solution of the problem
- Compromising, where both sides agree such that each wins or loses on certain significant issues
- Forcing, where the project manager uses his or her power to direct the solution, resulting in a type of win-lose agreement where

Copyright © Mometrix Media. You have been licensed one copy of this document for personal use only. Any other reproduction or redistribution is strictly prohibited. All rights reserved.

one side gets its way and the other does not

- Smoothing, where the major points of agreement are given the most attention and differences between the two sides are not highlighted and are thus not resolved
- Withdrawing, where one or both sides withdraw from conflict.

CONS - Disadvantages; an argument or opinion against something.

Consensual Management Style - Management approach in which the project manager presents problems to team members for discussion or input and encourages them to make decisions. This approach results in an increase in team member commitment to the group decision but also in the amount of time required to reach that decision.

Configuration Control - Process of maintaining the baseline identification and monitoring all changes to that baseline. Prevents unnecessary or marginal changes to the project scope while expediting the approval and implementation of changes that are considered needed or that offer significant project benefits.

Configuration Management - Process used to apply technical and administrative direction to document the functional and physical characteristics of an item or system, control any changes to the characteristics, record and report the changes and their implementation status, and audit the item or system to verify conformance to requirements. Approach used to control changes to these characteristics and provide information on the status of engineering or contract changes actions. Comprises three major areas of effort: configuration identification, configuration status accounting, and configuration control.

Conflict Management - Process by which an individual uses managerial techniques to deal with disagreements, both technical and personal in nature, that develop among the individuals working on the project.

Contingency Plan - Plan that identifies alternative strategies to be used if specified risk events occur. Examples include a contingency reverse in the budget, alternative schedule activity sequences, and emergency responses to reduce the impact of risk events.

Contract Administration - Management of the relationship with the contractor from contract award to closeout, focused specifically on ensuring that the contractor delivers a product or service in conformance with the contract's requirements.

Contract Work Breakdown Structure (CWBS) - Tool used to describe the total product and work to be done to satisfy a specific contract. Normally prepared by a contractor to reflect the statement of work in a specific contract or request for proposal. Used to define the level of reporting the contractor will provide the buyer.

Consensus - General accord. Each participant strongly agrees with the decision, or can live with it. Consensus is not reached if a participant strongly disagrees with the decision or cannot live with it.

Copyright © Mometrix Media. You have been licensed one copy of this document for personal use only. Any other reproduction or redistribution is strictly prohibited. All rights reserved.

Constraint - Restriction that affects the scope of the project, usually with regard to availability, assignment, or use of project cost, schedule, or resources. Any factors that affects when or how an activity can be scheduled. Any factor that limits the project team's options and can lead to pressure and resulting frustrations among team members.

Contingency - Provision for any project risk element within the project scope; particularly important when comparison of estimates and actual data suggests that certain risk events are likely to occur. If an allowance for escalation is included in the contingency, such should be a separate item, calculated to fit expected price level escalation conditions for project. Possible future action that may stem from presently known causes, the cost outcome of which cannot be determined accurately.

Corrective Action - Changes made to bring expected future performance of the project in line with the project plan.

Cost - Cash value of project activity; value associated with materials and resources expended to accomplish project objectives. Sum or equivalent that is expended, paid, or charged for something.

Cost Account - Defined work element or category for which actual costs can be accumulated and compared to BCWP. Cost category that represents the work assigned to one responsible organizational unit on a CWBS.

Control Account Plan (CAP) - Previously called a Cost Account Plan. The CAP is a management control point where the integration of scope and budget and schedule takes place, and where the measurement of performance will happen. CAPs are placed at selected management points of the work breakdown structure.

Controlling Processes - Actions taken by the project team to ensure that project objectives are met, by monitoring and measuring progress and taking corrective action when needed.

Consensus - General accord. Each participant strongly agrees with the decision, or can live with it. Consensus is not reached if a participant strongly disagrees with the decision or cannot live with it.

Cost Forecasting - Process of predicting future trends and cost throughout the project.

Cost Management - Function required to maintain effective financial control of the project by evaluating, estimating, budgeting, monitoring, analyzing, forecasting, and reporting cost information.

Cost Of Quality - Cost incurred or expended to ensure quality, including those associated with the cost of conformance and nonconformance.

Cost Overrun - Amount by which actual project cost exceed estimated costs.

Cost Baseline - Time-phased budget used to measure and monitor cost performance on the project. Developed by summing estimated cost by period and usually displayed in the form of an S-curve.

Cost Budgeting - Allocating cost estimates to individual project components.

Cost Center - Subdivision of an activity for which identification of cost is desired and through which costs can be controlled through one responsible manager.

Copyright © Mometrix Media. You have been licensed one copy of this document for personal use only. Any other reproduction or redistribution is strictly prohibited. All rights reserved.

Cost Estimating - Process of estimating the cost of the resources needed to complete project activities. Includes an economic evaluation, an assessment of project investment cost, and a forecast of future trends and costs.

Cost-Plus-Fixed Fee (CPFF) Contract - Type of contract in which the buyer reimburses the contractor for the contractor's allowable costs (as defined by the contract) plus a fixed amount of profit (fee). The fixed fee does not vary with actual cost but may be adjusted if changes occur in the work to be performed under the contract. In cost type contracts, the performance risk is borne mostly by the buyer, not the seller.

Cost-Plus-Incentive Fee (CPIF) Contract - Type of contract in which the buyer reimburses the contractor for the contractor's allowable costs (as defined by the contract) and the seller earns its fee (profit) if it meets defined performance or cost criteria. Specifies a target cost, target fee, minimum fee, maximum fee, and fee adjustment formula.

Cost-Plus-Percentage-Of-Cost (CPPC) Contract - Type of contract that provides reimbursement of allowable cost of services performed plus an agreed-upon percentage of the estimated cost as profits. In cost type contracts, the performance risk is borne mostly by the buyer, not the seller.

Cost Performance Index (CPI) - Ratio of budgeted cost to actual costs (BCWP / ACWP). Often used to predict the amount of a possible cost overrun or under run using the following formula: Commercial Projects CPI = P/A. Government Projects CPI = BCWP/ACWP

Cost Variance (CV) - Difference between the estimated and actual cost of an activity. In earned value, the numerical difference between BCWP and ACWP.

Cost-Plus-Award Fee (CPAF) Contract - Cost-reimbursement contract that provides for a fee that consists of a base fee (which may be zero) fixed at inception of the contract and an award fee based on periodic judgmental evaluation by the procuring authority. Used to provide motivation for performance in areas such as quality, timeliness, technical ingenuity, and cost-effective management during the contract. In cost type contracts, the performance risk is borne mostly by the buyer, not the seller.

Critical Activity - Activity on a critical path, commonly determined by using the critical path method.

Critical Path - In a project network diagram, the series of activities that determine the earliest completion of the project. Will change as activities are completed ahead of a behind schedule. Although normally calculated for the entire project, may also be determined for a milestone or subproject. Often defined as those activities with float less than or equal to specified value, often zero.

Critical Path Method (CPM) - Network analysis technique used to predict project duration by analyzing the sequence of activities (path) that has the least amount of scheduling flexibility (the least amount of float). Early dates are calculated by a forward pass using a specified start date. Late dates are calculated by a backward pass starting from a specified completion

Copyright © Mometrix Media. You have been licensed one copy of this document for personal use only. Any other reproduction or redistribution is strictly prohibited. All rights reserved.

date (usually the forward pass's calculated early finish date for the project).

Cost-Reimbursement Contract - Contract category that involves payment (reimbursement) to the contractor for its actual costs.

Crashing - Taking action to decrease the total project duration by adding resources (human and material) to the project schedule without altering the sequence of activities. The objective of crashing is to obtain the maximum duration compression for the least cost.

Criteria - A fact or standard by which judgments, decisions or actions are taken. Objectives, guidelines, procedures, and standards to be used for project development, design, or implementation.

Current Finish Date - Current estimate of the point in time when an activity will finish.

Current Start Date - Current estimate of the point in time when an activity will begin.

Customer Acceptance - Documented signoff by the customer that all project deliverables satisfy requirements.

Data Date (DD) - The date at which, or up to which, the project's reporting system has provided actual status and accomplishments. Also called as-of-date.

Critical Path Network (CPN) - Project plan consisting of activities and their logical relationship to one another. Out of the critical path method.

Critical Risk - Rick that can jeopardize achievement of project's cost, time, or performance objectives.

CRM-Computer Resource Management -

Cumulative Cost Curve - Graphic display used to show planned and actual expenditures to monitor cost variances. The difference in the height between the curves for planned expenditures and actual expenditures represents the monetary value of spending variance at any given time.

Deliverable - Measurable, tangible, verifiable outcome, result, or item that must be produced to complete a project or part of a project. Often used more narrowly in reference to an external deliverable, which is a deliverable that is subject to approval by the project sponsor or customer.

Delphi Estimating - The Delphi estimating technique uses a group of subject matter experts who develop estimates independently, discuss differences and assumptions, and go through one or more revision cycles, until a single estimate is agreed upon.

Delphi Technique - Form or participative expert judgment; an iterative, anonymous, interactive technique using survey methods to derive consensus on work estimates, approaches, and issues.

Decomposition - Subdivision of the major project deliverables into smaller, more manageable components until the deliverables are defined in sufficient detail to support future project activities (planning, executing, controlling, and closing).

Defect - Nonconformance of a characteristic with specified requirements, or a deficiency in something necessary for an item's intended, proper use.

Copyright © Mometrix Media. You have been licensed one copy of this document for personal use only. Any other reproduction or redistribution is strictly prohibited. All rights reserved.

Definitive Estimate - Used to develop the precise estimates needed to tactically manage and complete a project. The definitive estimate is the most accurate estimate for the amount of work and resources needed to complete the project. They are estimates consider to have a "+ or – 20%" accuracy. The definitive estimates are the estimates that the organization will commit to in order for the project to baseline; tactically manage the project or a major phase, and report performance against.

Design Specifications - Precise measurements, tolerances, materials, in-process and finished-product tests, quality control measures, inspection requirements, and other specific information that precisely describes how the work is to be done.

Detail Specifications - Written instructions detailing the objectives and design of an object.

Detailed Design - Output of system design; a technical or engineering description of a system that provides individual views of the system components; details on the physical layout of the system; and information on the system's individual applications, subsystems, and hardware components.

Democratic Management Style - Participative management approach in which the project manager and project team make decisions jointly.

Dependency - Logical relationship between and among tasks of project's WBS, which can be graphically depicted on a network diagram.

Dependent Tasks - Tasks that are related such that the beginning or end of one task is contingent on the beginning or end of another.

Design Review - Formal, documented, comprehensive, and systematic examination of a design to evaluate is capability to meet specified requirements, identify problems, and propose solutions.

Discipline - Area of technical expertise or specialty.

Discretionary Dependency - Dependency defined by preference, rather than necessity. Also called preferred logic, preferential logic, or soft logic.

Disruptive Management Style - Management approach, in which the project manager tends to destroy the unity of the team, be an agitator, and cause disorder on the project.

Document Control - System to control and execute project documentation in a uniform and orderly fashion.

Detailed Requirement - A requirement that describes the specific function that a particular product provides at a level of detail sufficient to support construction.

Development Methodology - Set of mutually supportive and integrated processes and procedures organized into a series of phases constituting the development cycle of a product or service.

Direct Project Costs - Costs directly attributable to a project, including all personnel, goods, or services and their associated costs, but not including indirect project costs, such as overhead and general office costs incurred in support of the project.

Direct Overhead - Portion of overhead cost that can be directly attributable to a project, such as rent, lighting and insurance.

Copyright © Mometrix Media. You have been licensed one copy of this document for personal use only. Any other reproduction or redistribution is strictly prohibited. All rights reserved.

Duration Compression - Shortening of the schedule without reducing the project scope. Often requires an increase in the project cost. Also called schedule compression.

Early Finish Date (EF) - Earliest possible point in time when the uncompleted portions of an activity (or the project) can end based on network logic and any schedule constraints. May change as the project progresses or as changes are made to the project plan. Used in the critical path method.

Early Start Date (ES) - Earliest possible point in time when the uncompleted portions of an activity (or the project) can begin based on network logic and any schedule constraints. May change as the project progresses or as changes are made to the project plan. Used in the critical path method.

Documentation - Collection of reports, information, records, references, and other project data for distribution and archival purposes.

DRM-Data Resource Management

Dummy Activity - Activity of zero duration that shows a logical relationship in the arrow diagramming method. Used when logical relationships cannot be completely or correctly described with regular activity arrows. Shown graphically as a dashed line headed by an arrow.

Duration (DU) - Number of work periods required to complete an activity or other project element. Usually expressed as hours, workdays, or workweeks. Sometimes incorrectly equated with elapsed time.

Enabling Product - A product which is not delivered to the customer or end user, but which is necessary to develop, support, maintain, or retire the end product.

End Product - Deliverable resulting from project work.

End user - Person or group for whom the project's product or service is developed.

End User Representative - A selected sample of end users who represent the total populations of end users.

Enhancement - Change or group of changes to the scope of an existing project that provides additional functionality, features, or capabilities.

Earned Value (EV) - Analysis of a project's schedule and financial progress as compared to the original plan.

Efficiency Factor - Ratio of standard performance time to actual performance, usually expressed as a percentage.

Effort - Number of labor units required to complete an activity or other project element. May be expressed as staff hours, days, or weeks. Should not be confused with duration.

Eighty-Hour Rule - Method of breaking down each project activity or task into work packages that require no more than 80 hours of effort to complete.

Elaborated - Worked out with care and detail; developed thoroughly.

Estimate To Complete (ETC) - Expected additional cost needed to complete an activity, group of activities, or the total project. Most techniques for forecasting ETC include an adjustment to the original based on project performance to date.

Estimating - Forecasting the cost, schedule, and resource requirements needed to produce a specific deliverable.

Copyright © Mometrix Media. You have been licensed one copy of this document for personal use only. Any other reproduction or redistribution is strictly prohibited. All rights reserved.

Event-On-Node - Network diagramming technique in which events are represented by boxes (or nodes) connected by arrows to show the sequence in which the events are to occur.

Exit Criteria - The conditions that must be satisfied before the process element is considered complete.

Enterprise - Company or organization. Subpart of a company or organization. Business of a customer.

Enterprise Project Management (EPM) - Comprehensive implementation and practice of project management based on the recognition that the sum total of an organization's work is a portfolio of simultaneous and interconnected projects that need to be managed collectively as well as individually.

Entry Criteria - The conditions that must be satisfied before an activity can be started.

Estimate At Completion (EAC) - Expected total cost of an activity, group of activities, or total project when the work is complete. Forecast of total project costs based on project performance to date. Three methods of calculating EAC; EAC = ACWP + ETC; BAC ÷ CPI; and ACWP + BCWS. Also called forecast at completion or latest revised estimate.

Expected Value - In risk management, results of multiplying the probability of a variable's occurrence with its estimated monetary impact. Although a theoretical figure, it provides some sense of the value of the loss incurred should the risk occur.

Expert Judgment - Opinions, advise, recommendations, or commentary proffered, usually upon request, by a person or persons recognized, either formally or informally, as having specialized knowledge or training in a specific area.

External Audit - Audit performed by anyone outside the project team.

External Dependency - Dependency that involves a relationship between project and non-project activities.

External Risk - Risk beyond the control or influence of the project team.

Exclusions - Items identified that are not to be included, which are kept out or omitted.

Executing Processes - Activities associated with coordinating people and other resources to implement the project plan.

Executive Management (OIS) - The group of OIS Managers collectively responsible for all of the OIS organizational units. Accountable for all Information Service (IS) initiatives, responsible to align IS with the business enterprise, exploits IS opportunities, manages IS-related risks appropriately, and ensures IS resources are used responsibly.

Expected Results - The desired outcome of a scenario defined in a test plan.

Feasibility Study - Examination of technical and cost data to determine the economics potential and practicality of project applications. Involves the use of techniques such as the time value of money so that projects may be evaluated and compared on an equivalent basis. Interest rates, present value factor, capitalization costs, operating costs, and depreciation are all considered.

Feedback - Information derived from observation of project activities, which is

Copyright © Mometrix Media. You have been licensed one copy of this document for personal use only. Any other reproduction or redistribution is strictly prohibited. All rights reserved.

used to analyze the status of the job and take corrective action if necessary.

Finish Date - Point in time associated with an activity's or project's completion. Usually qualified by terms such as actual, planned, estimated, scheduled, early, late, baseline, target, or current.

Finish-To-Finish (FF) - Relationship in precedence and diagramming method network in which one activity must end before the successor activity can end.

Facilitator - Person external to a group whose purpose is to help the group work more effectively.

Facilities Management Style - Management approach in which the project manager makes himself or herself available to answer questions and provide guidance when needed but does not interfere with day-to-day tasks.

Fast-Tracking - Compressing the project schedule by overlapping activities normally performed in sequence, such as design and construction. Sometimes confused with concurrent engineering.

Feasibility - Assessment of the capability for successful implementation; the possibility, probability, and suitability of accomplishment.

Fixed-Price Level-Of Effort Contract - Type of firm-fixed-price contract requiring the contractor to provide a specified level of effort over a stated period of time in work that can be stated only in general terms.

Fixed-Price-Contract - Type of contract with a firm pricing arrangement established by the parties at the time of contracting. A firm-fixed-price contract is not subject to adjustment on the basis of the contractor's cost experience in performing the contract. Other types of fixed-price contracts (fixed-price contract with economic price adjustment, fixed-price incentive contract, fixed-price re determination prospective contract, and fixed-price re determination retroactive contract) are subject to price adjustment on the basis of economic conditions or the contractor's performance of the contract.

Float - Amount of time that an activity may be delayed from its early start without delaying the project end date. Derived by subtracting the early start from the late start or early finish from the late finish, and may change as the project progresses and as changes are made to the project plan. Also called slack, total float, and path float.

Finish-To-Start (FS) - Relationship in a precedence diagramming method network in which one activity must end before the successor activity can start. The most commonly used relationship in the precedence diagramming method.

Firm-Fixed-Price (FFP) Contract - Type of contract in which the buyer pays the contractor a set amount (as defined by the contract) regardless of the contractor's costs. In the fixed-price contracts, the performance risk in borne mostly by the seller, not the buyer.

Fixed Cost - Cost that does not vary with volume of output.

Fixed-Price Incentive (FPI) Contract - Type of contract in which the buyer pays the contractor for the actual allowable cost incurred, not to exceed a ceiling price defined in the contract, and the contractor can earn more or less profit depending on its ability to meet defined performance or cost criteria. In fixed-price contracts, the

Copyright © Mometrix Media. You have been licensed one copy of this document for personal use only. Any other reproduction or redistribution is strictly prohibited. All rights reserved.

performance risk is borne mostly by the seller, not the buyer.

Forecasting - Estimating or predicting future conditions and events. Generally done during the planning process. Often confused with budgeting, this is a definitive allocation of resources rather than a prediction or estimate.

Formal Acceptance - Documentation signifying that the customer or sponsor has accepted the product on the project or phase. May be conditional if the acceptance is for a phase of the project.

Formal Authority - Influence based on an individual's position in the organization and conferred upon that person by the organization. Also called legitimate authority.

Formula Estimating - Method of work effort estimation using a prescribed method or formula to list and quantify major factors that impact project or product development.

Floating Task - Task that can be performed earlier or later in the schedule without affecting the project duration or critical path.

Flowchart - Diagram consisting of symbols depicting a physical process, a thought process, or an algorithm. Shows how the various elements of a system or process relate and which can be used for continuous process improvement.

Forecast - Estimate or prediction of future conditions and events based on information and knowledge available at the time of the estimate.

Forecast Estimating - Using a historical base of previous estimates or actuals and applying variables to determine a predictable estimate. The technique uses a forecasting algorithm, which includes variables and their impact, to the selected base data.

Functional Requirements - Characteristics of the deliverable described in ordinary, non-technical language that is understandable to the customer. Customer plays a major, direct role in their development.

Function-Point Analysis - Approach to estimating software costs that involves examining the project's initial high-level requirements statements, identifying specific functions, and estimating total cost based on the number of functions to be performed.

Gantt Chart - A Gantt Chart is a horizontal bar chart that graphically displays time relationships. In effect, it is a "scale" model of time because the bars are different lengths depending upon the amount of time they represent. It is named after Henry Laurence Gantt, the American engineer and social scientist who first developed it. Gantt charts have been around since the early 1900s and are frequently used in business to plan and manage large projects.

Forward Pass - Calculation of the early start and early finish dates for the uncompleted portions of all network activities.

Free Float - Amount of time that an activity may be delayed without delaying the early start of any immediately succeeding activities. Also called secondary float.

Functional Department - Specialized department within an organization that performs a particular function, such as

Copyright © Mometrix Media. You have been licensed one copy of this document for personal use only. Any other reproduction or redistribution is strictly prohibited. All rights reserved.

engineering, manufacturing, or marketing.

Functional Organization - Organizational structure in which staff is grouped hierarchically by specialty, such as production, marketing, engineering, and accounting at the top level, with each area further divided into sub areas. (For example, engineering can be subdivided into mechanical, electrical, and so on). Coordination is accomplished by functional "line" managers and upper levels of management.

Go/No Go - Major decision point in the project life cycle. Measure that allows a manager to decide whether to continue, change, or end an activity or project. Type of gauge that tells an inspector if an object's dimension is within certain limits.

Goal - Basic component for measuring progress in attaining project objectives.

Gold-Plating - Providing more than the customer or specifications require, and thus spending more time and money than necessary to achieve quality.

Grade - Category or rank given to items that have the same functional use but do not share the same requirements for quality; low quality is always a problem, but low grade may not be.

Gap Analysis - Examination of the difference between the current state and the desired or optimum state. Technique to help visualize the budget options available in project portfolios. Uses exploratory and normative forecasting and compares the curves associated with the total budget requirements of existing projects with that of the total anticipated budget for all projects, even those that are not under way. An anticipated gap can be determined and analyzed.

General And Administrative (G&A) Expense - Management, financial, or other expense incurred by or allocated to an organizational unit for the general management and administration of the organization as a whole.

General Management - Broad subject dealing with every aspect of managing an organization whose work is a continuous stream of activities. General management and project management share similar skills.

Generally Accepted - The knowledge and practices are applicable to most projects, most of the time, and that there is widespread consensus about their value and usefulness.

Hanger - Unintended break in a network path. Usually occurs as a result of missing activities or missing logical relationship.

Happy Path - A default scenario with no exceptional conditions.

Help Desk - Provides a single point of contact for customers to resolve PC/Mainframe hardware and software problems.

Herzberg's Theory Of Motivation - Theory of motivation developed by Fredrick Herzberg in which he asserts that individuals are affected by two opposing forms of motivation: hygiene factors and motivators. Hygiene factors such as pay, attitude of supervisor, and working conditions serve only to demotivate people if they are not provided in the type or amount required by the person. Improving hygiene factors under normal circumstances is not likely to increase motivation. Factors such as greater

Copyright © Mometrix Media. You have been licensed one copy of this document for personal use only. Any other reproduction or redistribution is strictly prohibited. All rights reserved.

freedom, more responsibility, and more recognition serve to enhance self-esteem and are considered the motivators that energize and stimulate the person to enhance performance.

Grapevine - Informal and unofficial communications path within an organization. Grapevine information has been shown to be accurate but usually incomplete.

Graphical Evaluation And Review Technique (GERT) - Network analysis technique that allows for conditional and probabilistic treatment of logical relationships (for example, some activities may not be performed).

Guideline - Document that recommends methods and procedures to be used to accomplish an objective.

Hammock - Group of related activities that is shown as one aggregate activity and reported at a summary level. May or may not have an internal sequence.

Histogram - Timeline chart that shows the use of a resource over time.

Historical Cost - Actual cost incurred in performing the work.

Historical Estimating - Method of estimating work efforts and costs using documented data past project or from similar tasks as the major input to the estimating process.

Human Resource Loading Chart - Vertical bar chart used to show personnel resource consumption by time period.

Heuristic - Problem-solving technique that results in an acceptable solution; often arrived at by trial and error.

Hierarchical Management - Traditional functional, or line, management in which areas and sub areas of expertise are created and staffed with human resources. Organizations so established are ongoing in nature.

High-Level Requirement - A requirement that broadly expresses a system-level response to a stakeholder need. High-level requirements usually need to be analyzed and refined with more detail.

High-Performance Work Teams - Group of people who work together in an interdependent manner such that their collective performance exceeds that which would be achieved by simply adding together their individual contributions. Characteristics of such a team include strong group identify, collaboration, anticipating and acting on other team members needs, and a laser-like focus on project objectives.

Indirect Cost - Cost not directly identified with one final cost objective. May be identified with two or more final or one or more intermediate cost objectives. Cost allocated to the project by the performing organization as a cost of doing business. Also called overhead cost or burden.

Information Distribution - Timely provision of needed information to project stakeholders in a variety of formats.

Information Requirement - Information needed to perform day-to-day operations.

Information System - Complex, interactive structure of people, equipment, processes, and procedures designed to produce information collected from both internal and external sources for use in decision-making activities.

Copyright © Mometrix Media. You have been licensed one copy of this document for personal use only. Any other reproduction or redistribution is strictly prohibited. All rights reserved.

Idle Time - Time interval during which the project team, equipment, or both, do not perform useful work.

Impact - Estimate of the effect that a risk will have on schedule, costs, product quality, safety, and performance.

Impact Analysis - Qualitative or quantitative assessment of the magnitude of loss or gain to be realized should a specific risk or opportunity event - or series of interdependent events-occurs.

Incremental Approach - Phased approach to project completion whereby certain project functionalities and capabilities are delivered in phases. Allows stakeholders to realize certain benefits earlier than if they were to wait for the total project to be completed.

Initiation - Process of formally recognizing that a new project exists or that an existing project should continue into its next phase.

Input - Information or other items required to begin a processes or activity. Documents or documentable items to be acted upon. Information, thoughts, or ideas used to assist in decision-making.

Inspection - Examination or measurement of work to verify whether an item or activity conforms to a specific requirement.

Integrated Project Plan - An integrated collection of documents that represents agreement and ensures that all the various elements of the work, costs, scope, and schedule are properly defined, resourced, coordinated, and managed. The plans represent a hierarchical breakdown of defined work, costs, resources, deliverables and agreed

quality, communication, change, budget, and risk controls.

Information Systems Steering Committee (ISSC) - The information technology (IT) strategic planning, policy and advocacy body for the DHS enterprise.

In-House - Work performed by one's own employees as opposed to an outside contractor.

Initial Project Plan - Top-down, high-level plan used to document the early approach to a project; usually contains resource manager commitments and a preliminary technical solution. Method for communication during the delegation of a project responsibility and acceptance of a project commitment.

Initiating Processes - Procedures for recognizing that a project or phase should begin and committing to start it.

Internal Audit - Self-audit conducted by members of the project team or a unit in the organization.

Internal Control - Process of monitoring and dealing with deviations from the project plan.

Internal Documentation - Written information that is associated with the development process, the quality system, and the product; is retained in the project files; and is not part of the final product.

Internal Risk - Risk under the control or influences of the project team.

International Standards Organization (ISO) - Voluntary organization consisting of national standardization bodies of each member country. Prepares and issues standards identified as "ISO-XXXX".

Integrated System Testing - When a modified system is processed in combination with other systems to ensure

Copyright © Mometrix Media. You have been licensed one copy of this document for personal use only. Any other reproduction or redistribution is strictly prohibited. All rights reserved.

it does not inadvertently cause changes in other systems.

Interdependencies - Relationship among organizational functions in which one function, task, or activity is dependent on others.

Interfaces - Boundary areas, often ill defined, between departments or functions.

Intermediate Estimate - The intermediate Estimate is used in support of a preliminary plan, a partial plan, or a plan that does not require precise estimating. Estimates developed to support the project plan in the early phases of the project, until a definitive estimate is needed or can be completed. An intermediate estimate is more precise than the ROM estimate, but not as precise as a definitive estimate. It is consider to be within "= or - 30%" accuracy.

Ishikawa Diagram - Diagram used to illustrate how various causes and sub causes create a specific effect. Named after its developer Kaoru Ishikawa. Also called cause-and effect diagram or fishbone diagram.

ISO-International Standards Organization. ISO 9000 - Set of documented standards to help organizations ensure that their quality systems meet certain minimal levels of consistent performance.

Issue - A point or matter of discussion, debate, or dispute. Formally identified item related to a project that, if not addressed, may-

- Affect its schedule
- Change its direction
- Diminish its quality
- Increase its cost

Distinguished from a risk in that it is an extant problem, whereas a risk is a future event. In many organizations, the terms are used interchangeably.

Intimidating Management Style - Management approach in which the manager frequently reprimands team members, to uphold his or her image as a demanding manger, at the risk of lowering team morale.

Invitation For Bid (IFB) - In U.S. federal government procurement, solicitation document used in sealed bidding procurements; generally, equivalent to a request for proposals.

Invoice - Written account or itemized statement addressed to the purchaser of merchandise shipped or services performed with the quality, prices, and charges listed. Contractor's bill or written request for payment for work or services performed under the contract.

IRM Plan (Information Resources Management Plan) - Integrated with the Business Plan, "the IRM Plan defines the goals, project plans, and technology needs for a specified biennium. The Plan also identifies the strategic technological direction for supporting and achieving future goals and objectives."

Key Stakeholder - A key stakeholder is a person who participates in the decision to approve or disapprove requirements on the behalf of other stakeholders

Kickoff Meeting - Meeting held to acquaint stakeholders with the project and each other; presumes the presence of the customer and serves as an initial review of the project scope and activities. Usually conducted after contract award or a decision to initiate a project.

Copyright © Mometrix Media. You have been licensed one copy of this document for personal use only. Any other reproduction or redistribution is strictly prohibited. All rights reserved.

Kinesics - Study of communication through body movement.

KISS Model - Pragmatic philosophy of conducting business in which the objective is to keep things, such as procedures, reports, and any other aspect of work, as simple as possible to get the job done. They acronym humorously describes the basic premise of simplicity, which is "keep it simple stupid".

Issue Management - Structured, documented, and formal processes or set of procedures used by an organization or a project to identify, categorize, and resolve issues.

JAD (Joint Application Development) - A structured, facilitated process for gathering and negotiating requirements.

Job Description - Written outline, by job type, of the skills, responsibilities, knowledge, authority, and relationships involved in an individual's job. Also called position description.

Judicial Management Style - Management approach in which the project manager exercises sound judgment and applies it to project issues as the need arises.

Lag Relationship - One of four types of relationships involving a lag between the start or finish of a work item and the start or finish of another work item:

- Finish-to-start
- Start-to-finish
- Finish-to-finish and
- Start-to-start

Laissez-Faire Management Style - Management approach in which team members are not directed by management. Little information flows from the project team to the project manager, or vice versa. This style is appropriate if the team is highly skilled and knowledgeable and wants no interference by the project manager.

Late Finish Date (LF) - Latest possible point in time that an activity may end without a delay in the project finish date. Used in the critical path method.

Knowledge Transfer - Flow of knowledge, skills, information, and competencies from one person to another. Can happen through any number of methods including coaching, mentoring, training courses and on-the-job experience.

Labor - Effort expended by people for wages or salary. Generally classified as either direct or indirect. Direct labor is applied to meeting project objectives and is a principal element used in costing, pricing, and profit determination; indirect labor is a component of indirect cost, such as overhead or general and administrative costs.

Labor Efficiency - Ratio of earned hours to actual hours spent on a prescribed task during a reporting period. When earned hours equal actual hours, the efficiency equals 100 percent.

Lag - Modification of a logical relationship in a schedule such that there is a delay in the successor task. For example, in a finish-to-start dependency with 5-day lag, the successor activity cannot start until 5 days after the predecessor has finished.

Leader - Individual who uses his or her influence in a group to motivate others to do something. Often used to refer to the project manager who is the individual vested with formal authority for achieving project aims.

Leadership - Use of influence to direct the activity of others towards the

Copyright © Mometrix Media. You have been licensed one copy of this document for personal use only. Any other reproduction or redistribution is strictly prohibited. All rights reserved.

accomplishment of some objective. Ability to persuade others to do things enthusiastically. Human factor that binds a group together and motivates it toward goals.

Leading - Establishing direction and aligning, motivating, and inspiring people.

Learning Curve - Graphical or numerical relationship between the average cost or unit cost of an item and the quantity produced. Tool used to project the amount of direct labor or material that will be used to manufacture a product on a repetitive basis.

Late Start Date (LS) - Latest possible points in time that an activity may begin without delaying the project finish date. Used in the critical path method.

Law Of Diminishing Returns - Economics theory stating that beyond a certain production or quality level, productivity or quality increases at a decreasing rate. Therefore, for every dollar invested in efforts to increase productivity, or quality, one can expect less than a dollar of productivity or quality gains in return.

Lead - Modification of a logical relationship in a schedule such that there is an acceleration of the successor task. For example, in a finish-to-start dependency with a 5-day lead, the successor activity can start 5 days before the predecessor has finished.

Lead Time - The time required to wait for a product, service, material, or resources, after ordering or making a request for such things.

Life Cycle - The entire useful life of a product or service.

Life-Cycle Cost - The sum total of all costs associated with the life cycle, including

developing, acquiring, operating, supporting, and (if applicable) disposing of the product or service developed or acquired so decisions can be made among alternatives.

Line Function - That part of a corporation that is responsible for producing its goods or performing its services.

Line Manager - Manager of a group that makes a product or performs a service. Also called functional manager.

Lessons Learned - Documented information, usually collected through meetings, discussions, or written reports, to show how both common and uncommon project events were addressed. The information can be used by other project managers as a reference for subsequent project efforts.

Level Of Approval - Management level at which approvals are given.

Level Of Effort (LOE) - Support-type activity (such as vendor or customer liaison) that does not readily lend itself to measurement of discrete accomplishment and is generally characterized by a uniform rate of activity over a specific time period.

Lose-Lose - Outcome of conflict resolution that results in both parties being worse off than before. Based on the strategy that it is better for each party to get something than nothing, even if that something does not accomplish either party's goals.

Lowest Overall Cost - Considering price and other factors, the least expenditure of funds over the life cycle of a system or an item.

Maintenance - The modification of a software product, after delivery, to correct faults, to improve performance or

Copyright © Mometrix Media. You have been licensed one copy of this document for personal use only. Any other reproduction or redistribution is strictly prohibited. All rights reserved.

other attributes, or to adapt the product to a changed environment.

Maintenance Guarantee - Assurance that a product will be maintained during a specified period of time.

Make-Or-Buy Analysis - Management technique used to determine whether a particular product or service can be produced or performed cost-effectively by the performing organization or should be contracted out to another organization. The analysis considers both the direct costs of procuring the product or service and any administrative costs in managing the contractor.

Linked Activity - Activity dependent on the performance of another activity in precedence diagramming.

Loaded Rates - Charges for human and material resources that incorporate both hourly or per-use charges and all additional general and administrative costs associated with their use.

Logical Relationship - Dependency between two project activities or between a project activity and a milestone. The four types of logical relationships in the precedence diagramming method are:

- Finish-to-start - the "from" activity must finish before the "to" activity can start
- Finish-to-finish - the "from" activity must finish before the "to" activity can finish,
- Start-to-start- the "from" activity must start before the "to" activity can start, and
- Start-to-finish - the "from" activity must start before the "to" activity can finish

Loop - Network path that passes the same node twice. Loops cannot be analyzed using network analysis techniques such CPM and PERT but are allowed in GERT.

Management By Projects - Management approach that treats many aspects of ongoing operations in an organization as projects, applying project management principles and practices to them.

Management Reserve - Separately planned quantity of money or time intended to reduce the impact of missed cost, schedule, or performance objectives, which are impossible to plan for (sometimes called "unknown unknowns").

Management Style - One of the following management approaches that a project manager may adopt depending on the situation: authoritarian autocratic, combative, conciliatory, consensual, consultative-autocratic, democratic, disruptive, ethical, facilitating, intimidating, judicial, laissez-faire, participative, promotional, secretive, shared leadership, or shareholder manger style.

Malcolm Baldrige National Quality Award - Established by the U.S. Department of Commerce and administered by the National Institute of Standards and Technology, this award is presented annually to U.S. corporations in various categories that have demonstrated a commitment to quality. Nominees complete a detailed application that solicits specific information regarding their quality activities in the following categories: leadership; strategic planning; customer and market focus; information and analysis; human resource focus;

Copyright © Mometrix Media. You have been licensed one copy of this document for personal use only. Any other reproduction or redistribution is strictly prohibited. All rights reserved.

process management; and business results.

Management By Exception - Management approach in which managers concern themselves with only those variances that appear exceptionally large, significant, or otherwise peculiar.

Management By objective (MBO) - Management approach or methodology, developed by Peter Drucker in the early 1950s that encourage managers to give their subordinates more freedom in determining how to achieve specific objectives. Management and the subordinate jointly develop clear objectives, requirements, and milestones and ensure that they are realistic, measurable, and achievable. Subordinate performance and compensation are measured by progress achieved against these goals at regular intervals.

Maturity Level - A defined position in an achievement scale that establishes the attainment of certain capabilities.

McGregor's Theory X and Y - Theory of motivation advanced by Douglas McGregor, which holds that managers have a tendency to hold two bipolar sets of assumption about workers. Theory X managers view workers as machines who require a great deal of external control. Theory Y managers view workers as organisms who grow, develop, and exercise control over themselves.

Measurement - The dimension, capacity, quantity, or amount of something (e.g., lines of code).

Mediation - Process of brining parties engaged in a dispute or disagreement together to settle their differences through a meeting with disinterested party, the mediator. Unlike binding arbitration, the mediator has no authority to force a settlement.

Mandatory Dependency - Dependency inherent in the nature of the work being done, such as a physical limitation. Also called hard logic.

Mandatory Requirements - Elements that must be included in the enhancement, without which success on the project will not be attained.

Maslow's Hierarchy Of Needs - Theory of motivation developed by Abraham Maslow in which a person's needs arise in an ordered sequence in the following five categories; (1) physical needs, (2) safety needs, (3) love needs, (4) esteem needs, and (5) self-actualization needs.

Matrix Organization - Project organizational structure in which the project manger shares responsibility with the functional mangers to assign priorities and direct the work of individuals assigned to the project. In a strong matrix organization, the balance of power over the resources is in favor of the project manager. In a weak matrix organization, functional mangers retain most of the control over project resources.

Milestone Schedule - Schedule consisting of key events or milestones (generally, critical accomplishments planned at time intervals throughout the project) and used to monitor overall project performance. May be either a network or bar chart and usually contains minimal detail at a highly summarized level.

Mission - Specific purpose that all or part of the organization is dedicated to achieving.

Copyright © Mometrix Media. You have been licensed one copy of this document for personal use only. Any other reproduction or redistribution is strictly prohibited. All rights reserved.

Mission Statement - Description prepared and endorsed by members of the organization that answers these questions: What do we do? For whom do we do it? How do we go about it? Used as a guide for making decisions in projects.

Mitigation - Carefully organized steps taken to reduce or eliminate the probability of a risk's occurring or the impact of a risk on a project.

Milestone - Event with zero duration and requiring no resources, used to measure the progress of a project signifies completion or start of a major deliverable or other significant metric such as cost incurred, hours used, payment made, and so on. Identifiable point in a project or set of activities that represents a reporting requirement or completion of a large or important set of activities.

Milestone Chart - Scheduling technique used to show the start and completion of milestone on a time-scale chart. Normally, planned events are expressed using hollow triangles, and completed events are shown as solid triangle. Rescheduled or slipped events are usually displayed as hollow diamond symbols. When the late milestones are completed, the diamonds are filled in.

Milestone Method - Approach to calculating earned value, which works well when work package exceed 3 months in duration. First, objective milestones are established, preferably one or more for each month of the project. Then, the assigned work package budget is divided, based on a weighted value assigned to each milestone.

Monitor - Acquire and analyze data on an ongoing basis so that action can be taken when progress fails to match plans and meet objectives.

Monte Carlo Analysis - Schedule or cost risk assessment technique that entails performing a project simulation many times to calculate a likely distribution of result.

Most Likely Time - In PERT estimating, the most realistic number of work periods the activity will consume.

Motivating - Inducing an individual to work towards his or her goals.

Mitigation Strategy - Carefully organized steps taken to reduce or eliminate the probability of a risk's occurring or the impact of a risk on a project.

Mixed Organization - Organizational structure that includes both functions (disciplines) and project in its hierarchy.

Model - Way to look at an item, generally by abstracting and simplifying it to make it understandable in a particular context.

Modification - Change to a project's scope or the terms of a contract; usually written. Examples are changes orders, notices of termination, supplemental agreements, and exercises of contract options.

Myers-Briggs Type Indicator - Test developed by Katherine C. Briggs and Isabel Briggs Myers to categorize people according to where they lie on four scales, each reflecting a different dimension of human behavior: extrovert-introvert, sensing-intuitive, thinking-feeling, and judging-perceiving. These scales comprise 16 different psychological types, each associated with a number of well-documented behavioral traits.

Necessary Requirement - An essential capability, physical characteristic or quality factor. Deletion of the

- 81 -

Copyright © Mometrix Media. You have been licensed one copy of this document for personal use only. Any other reproduction or redistribution is strictly prohibited. All rights reserved.

requirement would cause an unacceptable deficiency in the system.

Negative Float - Situation in which the difference between the late (start of finish) date and early (start or finish) date of an activity is a negative number, indicating that the late date is earlier in time than the early date. This situation comes into existence when a forced end date of an activity is used to calculate the backward pass without considering the predecessor activity's start date and duration. Negative float means the activity cannot be completed on time unless and until certain decisions are made to correct the situation.

Motivation-Hygiene Theory - Theory of motivation described by Frederick's Herzberg, which asserts that two sets of factors must be considered to satisfy a person's needs:

- Those related to job satisfaction (motivators) and
- Those related to job dissatisfaction (hygiene or maintenance factors). To retain employees, managers must focus on improving negative hygiene factors (such as pay), but to get employees to devote a higher level of energy to their work, managers must use motivators (such as recognition).

Multidisciplinary - Encompassing effort by many types of people representing different skills and backgrounds in the organization.

Multiple-Project Scheduling - Process of developing a project schedule based on constraints imposed by other project.

Myers-Briggs Type Indicator

Network-Based Scheduling - Process of determining logical relationships among WBS work packages, activities, and tasks and then arranging same to establish the shortest possible project duration. Examples of these techniques include PERT, CPM, PDM.

Node - Junction point joined to some or all of the other dependency lines in a network; an intersection of two or more lines or arrows.

Nonconformance - Deficiency in characteristics, documentation, or procedures that makes the quality of material, service, or product unacceptable or indeterminate.

Objective - End toward which effort is directed; a predetermined result. Organizational performance criteria to be achieved and measured in the use of organizational resources.

Net Present Value (NPV) - Financial calculation that takes into account the times values of stream of income and expenditures at a given interest rate.

Network - Graphic depiction of the relationships of project work (activities or tasks). Communication facility that connects end systems; interconnected series of points, nodes, or situations connected by communication channels; or assembly of equipment through which connections are made between data stations.

Network Analysis - Identification of early and late start and finish dates for uncompleted portions of project activities. Also called schedule analysis.

Network Diagram - Schematic display of the logical relationship of project activities, usually drawn from left to right

Copyright © Mometrix Media. You have been licensed one copy of this document for personal use only. Any other reproduction or redistribution is strictly prohibited. All rights reserved.

to reflect project chronology. Also called logic diagram and often incorrectly referred to a PERT chart.

Optional Requirements - Elements that would enhance the system being modified, but if left out, success of the request(s) would still be attained.

Order-Of-Magnitude Estimate - Approximate estimate that is accurate to within -25 to +75 percent and is made without detailed data. Usually produced from a cost capacity curve, with scale-up or scale-down factors that are appropriately escalated and approximate cost capacity ratios. Used in the formative stages of an expenditure program for initial project evaluation. Also called preliminary, conceptual, or feasibility estimate.

Organization Chart - Graphic display of reporting relationship that provides a general framework of the organization.

Organizational Breakdown Structure (OBS) - Tool used to show the work units or work packages that are assigned to specific organizational units.

Objective - high level statement of the goal(s) of the project.

Open-Door Policy - nagement approach that encourages employees to speak freely and regularly to management regarding any aspect of the business or product. Adopted to promote the open flow of communication and to increase the success of business operations or project performance by soliciting the ideas of employees. Tends to minimize personnel problems and employee dissatisfaction.

Opportunity - Future event or series of events that, if occulting, will have a positive impact on the project. Benefit to be realized from undertaking a project.

Opportunity Cost - Rate of return that would have been earned by selecting an alternative project rather than the one selected. Opportunity cost is used as one variable in project selection.

Optimistic Time - In PERT estimating, the minimum number of work periods the activity will consume.

Outsourcing - Process of awarding a contract or otherwise entering into an agreement with a third party, usually a supplier, to perform services that are currently being performed by an organization's employees. Reasons:

- The service can be performed cheaper, faster, or better by a third party.
- The service (for example, janitorial services) is not a core business functions contributing to the revenue growth and technical expertise of the organization. Accordingly, management does not want to focus time and attention on it.

Overall Change Control - Activities concerned with influencing the factors that create changes to ensure that they are beneficial, determining that a change has occurred, and managing the actual changes when and as they occur. Coordination of changes across the entire project.

Overhead Rate - Percentage rate determined by dividing an organization's indirect cost pool for an accounting period by the base used to allocate indirect costs to work accomplished during the period of performance.

Copyright © Mometrix Media. You have been licensed one copy of this document for personal use only. Any other reproduction or redistribution is strictly prohibited. All rights reserved.

Organizational Planning - Process of identifying, documenting, and assigning project roles, responsibilities, and reporting relationships.

Organizational Resources - Human and nonhuman resources available to the organization to fulfill its mission, objectives, and goals.

Other Managers - Managers whose individuals and/or groups are involved in or may be affected by project activities.

Output - Documents or deliverable items that are a result of a process.

Pareto's Law - Principle, espoused by Joseph Juran and based on the work of nineteenth century Italian economist Vilfredo Pareto, stating that a relatively small number of causes typically will produce a large majority of problems or defects. Improvement efforts are usually most cost-effective when focused on a few high-impact causes.

Participative Management Style - Management approach in which the project manager solicits information from and shares decision-making with the project team.

Path - Set of sequentially connected tasks, activities, lines, or nodes in a project network diagram.

Path Convergence - Point at which parallel paths of a series of activities meet. Notable because of the tendency to delay the completion of the milestone where the paths meet.

Parallel Tasks - Independent tasks that proceed concurrently.

Parametric Cost Estimating - An estimating technique that uses a statistical relationship between data and other variables to calculate an estimate.

Put simply it uses a mathematical model to create the estimate. It typically uses percentage based estimating as the basis for the mathematical model.

Pareto Diagram - Histogram, ordered by frequency of occurrence, that shows the number of results that were generated by each identified cause. Usually includes a second scale to reflect percentage of results for each cause.

Performance Reporting - Collecting and disseminating information about project performance to provide project stakeholders with information about how resources are being used to achieve project objectives. Includes status reporting, progress reporting, and forecasting.

Performance Review - Meeting held periodically to access project status or progress.

Performing Organization - The organization primarily responsible to manage the work, budget, and other resources, to create and deliver the product or service.

PERT Chart - Specific type of project network diagram.

PERT formula - Program Evaluation And Review Technique (PERT) is an event-oriented, probability-based network analysis technique used to estimate project duration when there is a high degree of uncertainty with the individual activity duration estimates. PERT applies the critical path method to a weighted average duration estimate. The formula is as follows:

Copyright © Mometrix Media. You have been licensed one copy of this document for personal use only. Any other reproduction or redistribution is strictly prohibited. All rights reserved.

$$\frac{O + 4(ML) + P}{6}$$

Where O = optimistic time, ML = most likely time, and P = pessimistic time.

Pessimistic Duration - In PERT estimating, the maximum number of work periods the activity will consume. Also called pessimistic time.

Peer Audit - Audit conducted by a group of peers rather than full-time or assigned auditors.

Peer Review - Review of a project or phase of a project by individuals with equivalent knowledge and background who are not currently members of the project team and have not participated in the development of the project.

Percent Complete (PC) - Estimate, expressed as a percent, of the amount of work completed on an activity or group of activities, typically based on resource use. Used in calculating earned value.

Percentage Based Estimating - A technique that uses typical project phases and gives each phase the industry or known standard percentage of the overall project. I.e., Initiating=5%, Planning=15%, Execution=50%, Controlling=20%, and Closing=10%. Then, if the execution phase can be accurately estimated in effort hours with a high level of confidence, the other phases can be calculated based on the total hours estimated for execution representing 50% of the project. If the execution phase cannot be estimated with a high level of confidence, it is broken into activities, and the same logic is applied. The point is to estimate a piece of the project with a high level of confidence and use this estimate to calculate based on percentages.

Planned Activity - Activity or task that has not started or finished prior to the current date.

Planned Value (PV) - The physical work scheduled, plus the authorized budget to accomplish the scheduled work. Previously, this was called the budgeted costs for work scheduled (BCWS).

Planning Processes - Activities associated with devising and maintaining a workable scheme to accomplish the business need that the project was undertaken to address.

Platform - The hardware and systems software on which applications software is developed or installed and operated.

Product Description - The product description documents the characteristics of the product or service that the project is to create.

Phased Planning - Approach used to plan only to the level of detail that is known at the time. The output of each project phase includes a phase plan and an updated project plan. The phase plan is prepared at the task or work package level and provides the detailed work to be done in the next phase of the project; the updated project plan is the overall plan for the remainder of the project.

Plan (Project Plan) - "Project Plan" means an integrated collection of documents that represents agreement and ensures that all the various elements of the work, costs, scope, and schedule are properly defined, resourced, coordinated, and managed. The plans represent a hierarchical breakdown of defined work,

Copyright © Mometrix Media. You have been licensed one copy of this document for personal use only. Any other reproduction or redistribution is strictly prohibited. All rights reserved.

costs, resources, deliverables and agreed quality, communication, change, budget, and risk controls.

Plan-Do-Check-Act (PDCA) Cycle - Universal improvement methodology, advanced by W. Edwards Deming and based on the work of Walter Shewhart, designed to continually improve the processes by which an organization produces a product or delivers a service.

Price - Monetary amount paid, received, or asked in exchange for supplies or services, which is expressed as a single item or unit of measure for the supplies or services.

Probability - Likelihood of occurrence. Ratio of the number of chances that an event may or may not happen to the sum of the chances of both happening and not happening.

Probability Analysis - Risk quantification technique that entails specifying a probability distribution for each variable and then calculating values for situations in which any one or all of the variables are changed at the same time.

Problem Definition - Process of distinguishing between causes and symptoms to determine the scope of effort to pursue on the project.

Precedence Diagramming Method (PDM) - Network diagramming technique in which activities are represented by boxes (or nodes) and linked by precedence relationship lines to show the sequence in which the activities are to be performed. The nodes are connected with arrows to show the dependencies. Four types of relationships are possible: finish-to-finish, finish-to-start, start-to-finish, and start-to-start. Also called activity-on-node (AON) or activity-on-arc.

Predecessor Activity - Activity or task that must begin or end before another activity or task can begin or end. In ADM, the activity that enters a node. In PDM, the "from" activity.

Present Value - Value in current monetary units of work to be performed in the future. Determined by discounting the future price of the work by a rate commensurate with the interest rate on the funds for the period before payment is required.

Procurement Management Plan - Document that describes the management of the procurement processes, from solicitation planning through contract closeout.

Procurement Planning - Process to determine what and when to procure.

Product - End result of a project or a specific task, activity, or process; either a tangible, physical product or a clearly specified event.

Product Breakdown Structure - Hierarchical structure used to decompose the product into constituent parts, as in a Bill of Materials.

Procedures - Step-by-step instructions on ways to perform a given task or activity; may be accompanied by a statement of purpose and policy for a task, examples of the results of the task, and so forth. Prescribed method to perform specified work.

Process - Series of actions, steps, or procedures leading to a result. High-level sequence or flow of tasks performed during production of a product or delivery of a service.

Copyright © Mometrix Media. You have been licensed one copy of this document for personal use only. Any other reproduction or redistribution is strictly prohibited. All rights reserved.

Process Definition - Dividing a process into its component parts so that it may be described in detail.

Process Model - Approach to show how processes are linked together in a business unit.

Product Oriented Processes - Processes concerned with specifying and creating the project product. In the IS industry they are referred to as the Development Lifecycle processes.

Product Scope - Features, functions, and characteristics to be included in a product.

Program - Group of related projects managed in a coordinated way to obtain benefits not available from managing the projects individually; may include an element of ongoing activities or tasks.

Product Description - Documentation delineating the product characteristics or service hat the project is to create.

Product Development Process - Structured, organized, and usually documented approach that organizations follow to design, develop, and introduce new products to the marketplace. Stages include, concept, selection, design, development, testing, availability, and maintenance.

Product Documentation - Written information about the product, which is a part of the final work product.

Product Life Cycle - Total period of time that a product exists in the marketplace, from concept to termination.

Program Management - Management of a related series of project over a period of time, to accomplish broad goals to which the individual projects contribute.

Program Manager - Individual typically responsible for a number of related projects, each with its own project manager.

Project - A project is a temporary endeavor undertaken to create a unique product or service. It is an organized effort representing a level of commitment and ability to deliver a defined product or service to the customer within an agreed cost and/or time constraint. A piece of work rated using the business and technical assessment of low, medium, or high is considered a project.

Project Charter - Document issued by senior management that gives the project manager authority to apply organizational resources to project activities and formally recognizes the existence of a project.

Project Cost Estimate- The term "project cost estimate", as used during the project development process, includes all capital outlay costs, including right of way, structures and landscaping, but does not normally includes capital outlay support costs. There are two categories of project cost estimates: Project Planning Cost Estimates and Project Design Cost Estimates. Project Planning Cost Estimates are used for analysis of alternatives, approval, and for programming. Project Design Cost Estimates are used to summarize the cost of a Project's contract items of work.

Project Cost Management- Includes the processes required to ensure that the project is completed within an approved budget. The process includes: Cost estimating: Developing an approximation or estimate of the costs of the resources

Copyright © Mometrix Media. You have been licensed one copy of this document for personal use only. Any other reproduction or redistribution is strictly prohibited. All rights reserved.

needed to complete a project. Cost budgeting: Allocating the overall cost estimate to individual work items to establish a baseline for measuring performance. Cost control: Controlling changes.

Project Duration- Elapsed time from the project start date to the project finish date.

Project Closeout - Process to provide for project acceptance by the project sponsor, completion of various project records, final revision and issue of documentation to reflect the "as-built" condition, and retention of essential project documentation.

Project Communications Management - Parts of project management that includes the processes needed to ensure proper collection, dissemination, storage, and disposition of project information. Consists of communication planning, information distribution, performance reporting, and administrative closure.

Project Control - Activities associated with making decisions about present and future project activities. Usually based on the identification and collection of project performance information with the intent of ensuring successful project completion.

Project Justification - Use of the business need or purpose that the project was undertaken to address to provide the basis for evaluating future investment trade-offs.

Project Leadership Team - The team that supports and facilitates the project. Four key leadership roles typically defined and agreed upon before the project starts the planning phase, are the project sponsor, the project steering committee, the

project manager, and in some cases the technical lead or team lead.

Project Management (PM) - Application of knowledge, skills, tools, and techniques to project activities to meet or exceed stakeholder needs and expectations from a project.

Project Evaluation - Periodic examination of a project to determine whether the objectives are being met. Conducted at regular intervals, such as the beginning or end of a major phase. May result in redirection of the project with decisions to change the scope, time, or cost baselines, for example, or terminate the project.

Project Finish Date - Latest calendar finish date of all activities on the project based on network or resource allocation process calculations.

Project Human Resource Management - Part of project management that includes the processes necessary to ensure effective use of the people involved with the project; consists of organizational planning, staff acquisition, and team development.

Project Management Processes - Series of actions that describe and organize the work of the project.

Project Management Professional (PMP) - Professional certification awarded by the Project Management Institute to individuals who have met the established minimum requirements in knowledge, education, experience, and service in the discipline of project management.

Project Management Team - Members of the project team who are directly involved in project management activities.

Copyright © Mometrix Media. You have been licensed one copy of this document for personal use only. Any other reproduction or redistribution is strictly prohibited. All rights reserved.

Project Management Controls - Processes or procedures designed to ensure that project performance information is collected, analyzed, and reviewed by appropriate stakeholders and used to decide any course of action to achieve the projects objectives. Examples include time tracking, scope change requests, and control gates.

Project Management Institute (PMI®), Inc. - A non-profit professional organization dedicated to advancing the state-of-the-art in the management of projects. The PMI is the largest organization, nationally and internationally, providing the ethical and professional standards applicable to practitioners of project management.

Project Management Office - The Project Management Office typically is the champion, facilitator, and keeper of project management process, discipline and best practices for an organization.

Project Office - The Project Office typically is utilized on large or highly complex projects to provide coordination and administration of the project. The project office normally is responsible for schedule development and maintenance, budget, cost, resource, and deliverable tracking and monitoring, communications, project files and facilities.

Project Personnel - Members of the project team directly employed on a project.

Project Phase - Collection of logically related project activities, usually resulting in the completion of a major deliverable. Collectively, the project phases compose the project life cycle.

Project Manager - The person responsible for completing the project on time, within budget and to an agreed scope. They are responsible for facilitating the project by using the project management processes, organizing the project, and managing the teamwork activities consistent with the approved work plan.

Project Network Diagram - A schematic display of a project's activities and the logical relationships or dependencies among them.

Project Objectives - Identified, expected results and benefits involved in successfully completing the project. Quantifiable criteria that must be met for the project to be considered successful. Project scope expressed in terms of output, required resources, and schedule.

Project Procurement Management - Part of a project management that includes the processes required to acquire supplies and services from outside the performing organization. Consists of procurement planning, solicitation planning, solicitation, source selection, contract administration, and contract closeout.

Project Quality Management - Part of project management that consists of processes required to ensure that the project will satisfy its objectives. Includes quality planning, quality assurance, and quality control.

Project Risk - Cumulative effect of probability of uncertain occurrences that may positively or negatively affect project objectives. Degree of exposure to negative events and their probable consequences (opposite of opportunity). Characterized by three factors: risk event, risk probability, and amount at stake.

Copyright © Mometrix Media. You have been licensed one copy of this document for personal use only. Any other reproduction or redistribution is strictly prohibited. All rights reserved.

Project Plan - Formal, approved document, in summarized or detailed form, used to guide both project execution and control. Documents planning assumptions and decisions facilitate communication among stakeholders, and documents approved scope, cost, and schedule baselines.

Project Plan Development - Compilation of the results of all other planning processes into a consistent, complete document.

Project Plan Execution - Completion of the project plan by performing the activities described therein.

Project Planning - Developing and maintaining the project plan. Identifying the project objectives, activities needed to complete the project, developing the facilitating controls, and resources and quantities required to carry out each activity or task within the project. Approach to determine how to begin, sustain, and end a project.

Project Sponsor - Person in an organization whose support and approval is required for a project to start and continue.

Project Stakeholder - Individual or organization who is actively involved in the project or whose interests may be affected, either positively or negatively, as a result of project execution or successful project completion. Also sometimes called party-at-interest.

Project Team - All people actively supporting or working on the project. The project team typically includes the Project Leadership Team, and all planned or active resources, including direct project staff, business staff, support group personnel, and contracted personnel.

Project Risk Management - That part of the project management that includes the processes involved with identifying, analyzing, and responding to project risk; consists of risk identification, risk quantification, risk response development, and risk response control.

Project Schedule - Planned dates to perform activities and meet milestones.

Project Scope Management - Part of project management that includes the processes required to ensure that the project includes all the work required, and only the work required, to successfully complete the project; consists of initiation, scope planning, scope definition, scope verification, and scope change control.

Prototype - Small or full-scale, and usually functioning, form of a newly developed product, which is used to evaluate the product design.

Purchase Order - Offer to buy certain supplies, services, or construction from sources based on specified terms and conditions.

Quality - Total characteristics of an entity or item that affect its ability to satisfy stated or implied needs. Conformance to requirements or specifications. Fitness for use.

Quality Assurance (QA) - Process of regularly evaluating overall project performance to provide confidence that the project will satisfy relevant quality standards. Organizational unit responsible for quality assurance efforts.

Copyright © Mometrix Media. You have been licensed one copy of this document for personal use only. Any other reproduction or redistribution is strictly prohibited. All rights reserved.

Project Time Management - Part of project management that includes processes required to ensure that the project is completed on time; consists of activity definition, activity sequencing, activity duration estimating, schedule development, and schedule control.

Project-Based Organization - Organization that derives its revenue primarily from performing projects for others.

Projectized Organization - Organizational structure in which resources are assigned full time to the project manager, who has complete authority to assign priorities and direct the work of people on the project.

PROS - Advantages: an argument or opinion for something.

Quality Management - Planning, organizing, staffing, coordinating, directing, and controlling activities of management with the objective of achieving the required quality. Overall management function involved in determining and implementing quality policy.

Quality Management Plan - Document that describes how the project management team will implement its quality policy. The quality management plan becomes part of the overall project plan and incorporates quality control, quality assurance, and project quality improvement procedures.

Quality Planning - Identifying the specific quality standards that are relevant to the project and determining how to satisfy them.

Quality Audit - Structured review of quality management activities to identify lessons learned and improves performance of the project or other projects within the organization.

Quality Control (QC) - This involves monitoring both the products and process, to determine if the project is meeting the quality standards and identifying ways to eliminate causes of unsatisfactory results.

Quality Control Measurements - Results of quality control testing and measures presented in a form for comparison and analysis.

Quality Improvement - Action taken to increase the effectiveness and efficiency of the project to provide added benefits to project stakeholders.

Recurring Cost - Production cost, such as labor and materials that varies with quantity produced, as distinguished from nonrecurring cost.

Remaining Duration (RDU) - The time needed to complete an activity.

Remaining Float (RF) - Difference between the early finish and the late finish date.

Request - An official statement for service, to fix a problem, to enhance an existing system or function, or to develop a new system or function.

Request For Proposals (RFP) - Type of bid document used to solicit proposals from prospective contractors for products or services. Used when items or services are of a complex nature and assumes that negotiation will take place between the buyer and the contractor.

Range Estimating - Range estimates allow for expressing risk or uncertainty in estimates by applying principles of statistical analysis and probability

Copyright © Mometrix Media. You have been licensed one copy of this document for personal use only. Any other reproduction or redistribution is strictly prohibited. All rights reserved.

distribution. This method supplies a range of values for the estimate rather than a single estimate.

Rebaselining - Establishing a new project baseline because of sweeping or significant changes in the project scope. Must be approved by all parties.

Record Retention - Period of time that records are kept for reference after contract of project closeout.

Records Management - Procedures established by an organization to identify, index, archive, and distribute all documentation associated with the project.

Reserve - Money or time provided for in the project plan to mitigate cost, schedule, or performance risk.

Resource Allocation - Process of assigning resources to the activities in a network while recognizing any resource constraints and requirements; adjusting activity level start and finish dates to conform to resource availability and use.

Resource Breakdown Structure (RBS) - Variation of the organizational breakdown structure used to show which work elements are assigned to individuals.

Resource Calendar - Calendar denoting when a resource or resource pool is available for work on a project.

Requirement - A statement or model identifying a capability, physical characteristic, or quality factor that bounds a need for which a solution will be pursued.

Requirements Definition - The first stage of software development, the process of reviewing a business's processes to determine the business needs and functional requirements that a system must meet.

Requirements Traceability - Process of understanding, documenting, approving, and auditing the relationships between a system's components and functions and the requirements from which the system was developed. Each function and component of a system should be directly traceable to a requirement identified by a user, client, customer, or stakeholder.

Requirements Traceability Matrix - A tabular format used to implement requirements traceability.

Resource Manager - The manager who is responsible for the staff, or who owns or controls the physical thing, that has been allocated to a project.

Resource Plan - Document used to describe the number of resources needed to accomplish the project work and the steps necessary to obtain a resource.

Resource Planning - Process of determining resources (people, equipment, materials) needed in specific quantities, and during specific time periods, to perform project activities.

Resource Pool - Collection of human and material resources that may be used concurrently on several projects.

Resource Histogram - Vertical bar chart used to show resource consumption by time period. Also called resource loading chart.

Resource Leveling - Practicing a form of network analysis in which scheduling decisions (start and finish dates) are driven by resource management issues (such as limited availability or changes in resource levels). Evening out the peaks and valleys of resource requirements so

Copyright © Mometrix Media. You have been licensed one copy of this document for personal use only. Any other reproduction or redistribution is strictly prohibited. All rights reserved.

that a fixed amount of resources can be used over time. Ensuring that a resource is maximized but not used beyond its limitations.

Resource Loading - Designating the amount and type of resources to be assigned to a specific activity in a certain time period.

Responsibility - Obligation of an individual or group to perform assignments effectively. Status of a prospective contractor that determines whether it is eligible for contract award.

Responsibility Assignment Matrix (RAM) - Structure used to relate the WBS to individual resources to ensure that each element of the project's scope of work is assigned to an individual. A high-level RAM defines which group or unit is responsible for each WBS element; a low-level RAM assigns roles and responsibilities for specific activities to particular people. Also called accountability matrix.

Responsibility - Obligation of an individual or group to perform assignments effectively.

Status of a prospective contractor that determines whether it is eligible for contract award.

Resource Requirements - Output of the resource planning process, which describes the types and quantities of resources required for each element of the WBS. Resources are then obtained through staff acquisition or procurement.

Resource-Constrained Scheduling - Special case of resource leveling where the start and finish dates of each activity are calculated based on the availability of a fixed quantity of resources.

Resource-Limited Schedule - Project schedule whose start and end dates for each activity have been established on the availability of a fixed and finite set of human and material resources.

Resources - People, equipment, or materials required or used to accomplish an activity. In certain applications, such things as "nonrainy days" are described as a resource.

Risk Appraisal - Work involved in identifying and assessing risk.

Risk Assessment - Review, examination, and judgment to see whether the identified risks are acceptable according to proposed actions. Identification and quantification of project risks to ensure that they are understood and can be prioritized. Also called risk evaluation.

Risk Description - Documentation of the risk element to identify the boundaries of the risk.

Risk Event - Discrete occurrence that may affect a project, positively or negatively.

Return On Investment (ROI) - Amount of gain, expressed as a percentage, earned on an organization's total capital; calculated by dividing total capital into earnings before interest, taxes, and dividends.

Reverse Scheduling - Method in which the project completion date is fixed and task duration and dependency information is used to compute the corresponding project start date.

Rework - Action taken to ensure that a defective or nonconforming item complies with requirements or specifications.

Risk Analysis - Analysis of the probability that certain undesirable and beneficial

Copyright © Mometrix Media. You have been licensed one copy of this document for personal use only. Any other reproduction or redistribution is strictly prohibited. All rights reserved.

events will occur and their impact on attaining project objectives.

Risk Prioritizing - Filtering, grouping, and ranking risks following assessment.

Risk Probability - Assessment of the likelihood that a risk event will occur.

Risk Quantification - Process of implementing risk strategies, documenting risk, and responding to changes in risk during the life of the project.

Risk Response Control - Process of implementing risk strategies, documenting risk, and responding to changes in risk during the life of the project.

Risk Exposure - Impact value of a risk multiplied by its probability of occurring. Loss provision made for a risk; requires that a sufficient number of situations in which this risk could occur have been analyzed.

Risk Factor - Risk event, risk probability, or amount at stake.

Risk Identification - Determining the risk events that are likely to affect the project and classifying them according to their cause of source.

Risk Management Plan - Documentation of the procedures to be used to manage risk during the life of a project and the parties responsible for managing various areas of risk. Includes procedures for performing risk identification and quantification, planning risk response, implementing contingency plans, allocating reserves, and documenting results.

ROM Estimate (Rough Order Of Magnitude) - A Rough Order of Magnitude (ROM) estimate is used for strategic

decisions and long range planning. It is an estimate, which is obtained based on very limited data. The ROM estimate is consider to have + or – 50% accuracy range. This method therefore supplies a range of values for the estimate rather than a single estimate.

Roster - A list of people's names and their contact information, often with their assigned roles or tasks.

Schedule - Time-sequenced plan of activities or tasks used to direct and control project execution. Usually shown as a milestone chart, Gantt or other bar chart, or tabular listing of dates.

Schedule Baseline - Approved project schedule that serves as the basis for measuring and reporting schedule performance.

Schedule Control - Management of project schedule changes.

Risk Response Development - Identification of specific actions to maximize the occurrence of opportunities and minimize the occurrence of specific risks in a project.

Risk Symptom - Indirect manifestation of an actual risk event, such as poor morale serving as an early warning signal of an impending schedule delay or cost overruns on early activities pointing to poor estimating.

Rolling Wave Planning - Progressive detailing of the project plan as necessary to control each subsequent project phase.

Risk Appraisal - Work involved in identifying and assessing risk.

Rollout - Widespread, phased introduction of a project's product or service into the organization.

Copyright © Mometrix Media. You have been licensed one copy of this document for personal use only. Any other reproduction or redistribution is strictly prohibited. All rights reserved.

Schedule Variance (SV) - Difference between the scheduled completion of an activity and its actual completion. In earned value, BCWP less BCWS; an SV of less than zero shows that project activity is behind schedule.

Scheduled Finish Date - Point in time when work is scheduled to finish on an activity; normally, between the early and late finish dates. Also called planned finish date.

Scheduled Start Date - Point in time when work is scheduled to start on an activity; normally, between the early and late start dates. Also called planned start date.

Scheduling - Fitting tasks into a logical timetable with detailed planning of work with respect to time. Determining when each item of preparation and execution must be performed.

Schedule Development - Analysis of activity sequences, activity durations, and resource requirements to prepare the project schedule.

Schedule Performance Index (SPI) - Analysis of activity sequences, activity durations, and resource requirements to prepare the project schedule.

Schedule Revision - Changes to the scheduled start and finish dates in the approved project schedule.

Schedule Risk - Risk that jeopardizes completing the project according to the approved schedule.

Schedule Update - Schedule revision to reflect the most current status of the project.

Scope Creep - Gradual progressive increase of the project's scope such that it is not noticed by the project management team or the customer. Occurs when the customer identifies additional, sometimes minor, requirements that, when added together, may collectively result in a significant scope change and cause cost and schedule overruns.

Scope Definition - Division of the major deliverables into smaller, more manageable components to:

- Improve the accuracy of cost, time, and resource estimates; A baseline for performance measurement and control; and
- Facilitate clear responsibility assignments

Scope Management Plan - Document that describes the management of project scope, integration of any scope changes into the project, and identification and classification of scope changes.

Scientific Wild Anatomical Guess (SWAG) - Estimate of time or cost of completing a project or element of work based solely on the experience of the estimator. Typically done in haste, SWAG estimates are usually no more accurate than order-of-magnitude estimates.

Scope - The sum of the products and services to be provided as a project.

Scope Change - Modification to the agreed-upon project scope as defined by the approved WBS.

Scope Change Control - Process of:

- Influencing the factors that cause scope changes to help ensure that the changes are beneficial,
- Determining that a scope change has occurred, and
- Managing the changes if and when they occur

Scope Constraint - Restriction affecting project scope.

Copyright © Mometrix Media. You have been licensed one copy of this document for personal use only. Any other reproduction or redistribution is strictly prohibited. All rights reserved.

S-Curve - Graphic display of cumulative costs, labor hours, or other quantities, plotted against time. The curve is flat at the beginning and end and steep in the middle. Generally describes a project that starts slowly, accelerates, and then tapers off.

Secretive Management Style - Management approach in which the project manager is neither open nor outgoing in speech, activity, or purpose, to the detriment of the project.

Shared Leadership Style - Management approach in which the project manager holds that leadership consists of many functions and that these can be shared among team members. Some common functions are time keeping, record keeping, planning, scheduling, and facilitating.

Scope Of Work - Description of the totality of work to be accomplished or resources to be supplied under a contract.

Scope Planning - Developing a written scope statement that includes the project justification, major deliverables, project objectives, and criteria used to determine whether the project or phase has been successfully completed.

Scope Statement - Documented description of the project concerning its output, approach, and content. Used to provide a documented basis to help make future project decisions and to confirm or develop a common understanding of the project's scope by stakeholders.

Scope Verification - Process of ensuring that all identified project deliverables have been completed satisfactorily.

Skills Assessment - A skill assessment collects and evaluates available skill levels and compares them to the required skills as defined by the needs assessment. This assessment, along with the needs assessment may be used to determine such things as training needs, time lines, and risks.

Software Engineering Institute (SEI) - U.S. government Federally Funded Research and Development Center (FFRDC), operated by Carnegie-Mellon University in Pittsburgh, Pennsylvania, under contract to the U.S. Department of Defense (DOD). SEI's mission is to improve software engineering processes for the DOD. Has become well-known worldwide for its software Capability Maturity Model (CMM), used by software development professionals to improve the processes by which they develop application programs.

Solicitation - Obtaining quotations, bids, offers, or proposals as appropriate. Document sent to prospective contractors requesting the submission of offers or information.

Short-Term Plan - Short-term schedule showing detailed activities and responsibilities for a particular period (usually 4 to 8 weeks). Management technique often used "as needed" or in a critical area of the project.

Significant Variance - Difference between the plan and actual performance that jeopardizes the project objectives.

Signoff - The "Approving Authority's" Authorization.

Six Sigma - Quality concept and aim developed by Motorola, Inc. and defined as a measure of goodness-the capability of a process to produce perfect work. Six sigma refers to the number of standard

Copyright © Mometrix Media. You have been licensed one copy of this document for personal use only. Any other reproduction or redistribution is strictly prohibited. All rights reserved.

deviations from the average setting of a process to the tolerance limit, which in statistical terms translates to 3.4 defects per million opportunities for error.

Specification - A definition of modifications to hardware and/or software.

Spiral Model - Progressive method of software development in which successive, more complete versions of the product are developed and verified only to be scrapped and replaced by a more complete and technically comprehensive version. This development approach usually involves close interaction and feedback with the ultimate end-user of the application program.

Sponsor - The individual or group who champions the project and provides the resources, in cash or in kind. Provides the executive leadership, priority and commitment to the project, its goals and objectives. This is the manager representing the organizational unit most affected by the business change. If several organizational units will be heavily impacted by the business change, this is an executive manager with authority over the majority of the organizational units.

Solicitation Planning - Documenting product or service requirements and identifying potential sources.

Span Of Control - Number of individuals (direct reports) that a manager or project manager can effectively manage. The number will vary, but generally, a manager should have no more than ten direct reports. Once that number is exceeded, the organizational structure needs to be reviewed and changed.

Specialist - Expert in a particular field who may be used as a resource for multiple projects in an organization.

Specification - Description of the technical requirements for a material, product, or service, including the criteria for determining that the requirements have been met. Generally, three types of specifications are used in projects: performance, functional, and design.

Stakeholders - Individuals and/or groups who are involved in or may be affected by project activities.

Standard -

- Basis for uniformly measuring or specifying performance.
- Document used to prescribe a specific consensus solution to a repetitive design, operations, or maintenance situation.
- Document approved by a recognized body that provides for common and repeated use, rules, guidelines, or characteristics for products, processes, or services; however, compliance is not mandatory.
- Documentation that establishes engineering and technical limitations and applications of items, materials, processes, methods, designs, and engineering practices.

Standard Procedure - Documented prescription that a certain type of work be done in the same way wherever it is performed.

Staff Acquisition - Process of obtaining the human resources needed to work on the project.

Copyright © Mometrix Media. You have been licensed one copy of this document for personal use only. Any other reproduction or redistribution is strictly prohibited. All rights reserved.

Staffing Management Plan - Document that describes when and how human resources will become part of the project team and when they will return to their organizational units; may be a part of the overall project plan.

Staffing Requirements - Determination of what kinds of skills are needed from what types of individuals or groups, how many, and in what time frames; a subset of the overall resource requirements.

Stakeholder Analysis - Assessment of project stakeholder information needs and sources and development of reporting procedures to meet those needs.

Statement Of Work (SOW) - Narrative description of products or services to be supplied under contract that states the specifications or other minimum requirements; quantities; performance dates, times, and locations, if applicable; and quality requirements. Serves as the basis for the contractor's response and as a baseline against which the progress and subsequent contractual changes are measured during contract performance.

Status Report - Description of where the project currently stands; part of the performance reporting process. Formal report on the input, issues, and actions resulting from a status meeting.

Steering Committee - The Steering Committee is the principal body, which represents the primary participating organizations or stakeholders. The representatives must be advocates, committed to ensuring that the project fulfills its stated objectives. The Steering Committee will assist the Sponsor in making key strategic decisions regarding the project and in resolving any issues that impact the representatives' organization's policy.

Start Date - Point in time associated with an activity's start. Usually qualified by one of the following terms: actual, planned, estimated, scheduled, early, late, target, baseline, or current.

Start-To-Finish - Relationship in a precedence diagramming method network in which one activity must start before the successor activity can finish.

Start-To-Start - Relationship in precedence diagramming method network n which one activity must start before the successor activity can start.

Structured Walkthrough - Systematic, comprehensive review of the requirements, design, or implementation of a system by a group of qualified experts.

Subnet - Subdivision of a project network diagram generally representing some form of subproject. Also called sub network or fragnet.

Subproject - Component of a project; often contracted out to an external enterprise or another functional unit in the performing organization.

Subtask - Portion of a task or work element.

Straight-Line Method Of Depreciation - Method in which an equal amount of an asset's cost is considered an expense for each year of its useful life.

Strategy - Action plan to set the direction for the coordinated use of resources through programs, projects, policies, procedures, and organizational design and establishment of performance standards.

Copyright © Mometrix Media. You have been licensed one copy of this document for personal use only. Any other reproduction or redistribution is strictly prohibited. All rights reserved.

Strengths- Weaknesses-Opportunities-Threats (SWOT) Analysis. Analysis used to determine where to apply special efforts to achieve desired outcomes. Entails listing:

- Strengths and how best to take advantage of them;
- Weaknesses and how to minimize their impacts;
- Opportunities presented by the project and how best to take advantage of them; and
- Threats and how to deal with them

Strong Matrix - Organizational structure in which the balance of power over resources shifts from the functional managers to the project manager and the project manager has greater decision-making influence.

SWAG-Silly Wild Ass Guess - A rough order of magnitude estimate given as a best guess by someone asked to give an estimate with very limited information about the work to be performed. A "SWAG" estimate can be expected to be off by, as much as, plus or minus fifty percent. For example a project estimated to take four months, may be completed in as little as two months or as much as six months.

System Architecture - Manner in which hardware or software is structured, that is, how the system or program is constructed, how its components fit together, and what protocols and interfaces are used for communication and cooperation among the components, including human interaction.

System Design - Translation of customer requirements into comprehensive, detailed functional, performance, or design specifications, which are then used to construct the specific solution.

Successor Activity - Activity that starts after the start of a current activity.

Sunk Costs - Costs that once expended can never be recovered or salvaged. Current thinking strongly suggests that sunk costs should not be considered a factor in deciding whether to terminate a project or allow it to continue to the next phase.

Support Staff - Individuals who provide assistance to the project team in areas, such as financial tracking and project administration.

System Testing - When a new or modified object is processed in combination with other objects to insure it works as part of the complete system.

Systems/Applications - A group of related components that interact to perform a task.

Target Date - Date an activity is planned to start or end. Date generated by the initial CPM schedule operation and resource allocation process.

Task - Well-defined component of project work; a discrete work item. There are usually multiple tasks for one activity.

Task Definition - Unique description of each project work division.

System Environment - The hardware and software platforms including development tools and databases, as well as the shop standards and styles, in which the system exists.

System Interfaces - Physical interfaces among connecting parts of a system, or performance interfaces among various functional or product subsystems.

Copyright © Mometrix Media. You have been licensed one copy of this document for personal use only. Any other reproduction or redistribution is strictly prohibited. All rights reserved.

System Life - Period of time that begins when an information technology application is installed and ends when the users' need for it disappears.

System Requirement - A condition or capability that must be met or possessed by a system to satisfy a condition or capability needed by a users.

Team Development - Development of individual and group skills to improve project performance. Enhancement of stakeholders' ability to contribute as individuals and to function as a team.

Technical Requirements - Description of the features of the deliverable in detailed technical terms to provide project team members with crucial guidance on what needs to be done on the project.

Technical Complexity - This represents the technical difficulty or risk associated with a particular business issue or opportunity that is driving a need for change.

Technical Project Leader - Person who serves primarily as the senior technical consultant on a team.

Task Type - Identification of a task by resource requirement, responsibility, discipline, jurisdiction, function, or any other characteristic used to categorize it.

Team Building - Planned and deliberate process of encouraging effective working relationships while diminishing difficulties or roadblocks that interfere with the team's competence and resourcefulness. Process of influencing a group of diverse people, each with individualized goals, needs, and perspectives, to work together effectively for the good of the project.

Team Building Activities - Management and individual actions undertaken specifically and primarily to improve team performance.

Test Scripts - A record of actions to be performed, expected results, and actual results used to test the effect of the modifications.

Theory W Management - Approach to software project management in which the project manager tries to make winners of each party involved in the software process. Its subsidiary principals are "plan the flight and fly the plan" and "identify and manage your risks."

Theory X Management - Approach to managing people described by MacGregor. Based on the philosophy that people dislike work, will avoid it if they can, and are interested only in monetary gain from their labor. Accordingly, the Theory X manager will act in an authoritarian manner directing each activity of his or her staff.

Technical Quality Support - Provision of technical training and expertise from one or more support groups to a project in a timely manner.

Technical Walkthrough - A thorough review of the object, using the detail specifications, test plan, test results, and shop standards, to ensure that the object construction is sound and meets the design.

Technique - Skilled means to an end.

Template - A guideline for a document outline and its contents. A template is used to record the work activities, discussions, findings, and specification to help achieve a common understanding. In addition it is used to provide a consistent

Copyright © Mometrix Media. You have been licensed one copy of this document for personal use only. Any other reproduction or redistribution is strictly prohibited. All rights reserved.

look and feel to the project documentation.

Thomas-Kilmann Conflict Mode Instrument - Questionnaire used to measure how much competing, collaborating, compromising, avoiding, and accommodating behavior is displayed in conflict situations. Examines the extent to which individuals focus on assertive versus cooperative behavior in work situations.

Threshold - Time, monetary unit, or resource level, placed on something, which is used as a guideline that, if exceeded, causes some type of management review to occur.

Tiger Team - Group of objective specialists, convened by management, who evaluates, assesses, and makes recommendations for resolving problems associated with a particular area of concern.

Tight Matrix - Physical placement of project team members in one location.

Theory Y Management - Approach to managing people described by MacGregor. Based on the philosophy that people will work best when they are properly rewarded and motivated, and that work is as natural as play or rest. Accordingly, the Theory Y manager will act in a generally supportive and understanding manner, providing encouragement and psychic rewards to his or her staff.

Theory Z Management - Approach to managing people described by Arthur and Ouchi. Based on the philosophy that people need goals and objectives, motivation, standards, the right to make mistakes, and the right to participate in goal setting. More specifically, describes a Japanese system of management characterized by the employee's heavy involvement in management, which has been shown to result in higher productivity levels when compared to U.S. or western counterparts. Successful implementation requires a comprehensive system of organizational and sociological rewards. Its developers assert that it can be used in any situation with equal success. Also called participative management style.

Timeline - A schedule showing a planned order or sequence of events and procedures.

Tolerance - Specific range in which a result is considered to be acceptable. Range of values above and below the estimated project cost, schedule, or performance within which the final value is likely to fall.

Tool Or Technique - A tool or techniques is a method that aids in achieving a desired result. For example, an estimating technique aids in developing the estimate. A tool or technique is typically not the only way to obtain the desired result but is one recommended method.

Top-Down Estimating - Cost estimating that begins with the top level of the WBS and then works down to successively lower levels. Also called analogous estimating.

Time Value Of Money - Economic concept which purports that money available now is more valuable than the same amount of money at some point in the future due simply to its potential earning power, and not inflation as many believe. Used in calculating the present value of money for

Copyright © Mometrix Media. You have been licensed one copy of this document for personal use only. Any other reproduction or redistribution is strictly prohibited. All rights reserved.

financial analysis as well as other purposes.

Time Variance - Scheduled time for the work completed less the actual time.

Time-Limited Scheduling - Scheduling activities so that the limits on resource use are not exceeded, unless those limits would push the project beyond its scheduled finish date. Activities may not begin later than their late start date, even if resource limits are exceeded. Should not be used on networks with negative total float time.

Traceability - Ability to trace the history, application, or location of an item or activity by means of recorded identification. - Ease with which a project can be traced forward from specifications to the final deliverable or backward from the deliverable to the original specifications in a systematic way.

Trade-Off - Giving up or accepting one advantage, or disadvantage, to gain another that has more value to the decision maker. For example, accepting the higher cost (a disadvantage) of a project because there will be more functionality (an advantage) in the delivered product.

Training - Activities designed to increase the skills, knowledge, and capabilities of the project team.

Total Cost - Sum of allowable direct and indirect costs that are allocable to the project and have been or will be incurred, less any allocable credits, plus any allocable costs of money.

Total Quality Management (TQM) - Approach used to achieve continuous improvement in an organization's processes and products. Common approach to implementing a quality improvement program within an organization. Philosophy and set of guiding principles that encourage employees to focus their attention on ways of improving effectiveness and efficiency in the organization.

Traceable - The origin of each requirement is clear and can be traced backward to the stakeholder need forward to other products.

Triple Constraint - Term used to identify what is generally regarded as the three most important factors that a project manager needs to consider in any project: time, cost and scope (specifications). Typically represented as a triangle, each of these constraints, when changed, will impact one or both of the others. They do not exist in isolation. For example, if the scope of a project increases, generally time and cost will also increase.

Unacceptable Risk - Exposure to risks that is significant enough to jeopardize an organization's strategy, present dangers to human lives, or represent a significant financial exposure, such that avoidance or mitigation is imperative.

Unallowable Cost - Cost incurred by a contractor that is not chargeable to the project on which the contractor is working.

Unit Test - A test of an object to see if remediation efforts were successful. The unit test does not test how well the object will work with the application and other applications.

Transformational Leadership - Motivational approach to management based on the philosophy and practice of encouraging employees to achieve greater

Copyright © Mometrix Media. You have been licensed one copy of this document for personal use only. Any other reproduction or redistribution is strictly prohibited. All rights reserved.

performance through inspirational leadership. Such an approach is thought to develop employee self-confidence and result in higher achievement goals.

Trend - A general inclination or tendency. A prevailing direction.

Trend Analysis - Use of mathematical techniques to forecast future outcomes based on historical results. Often used to monitor technical, cost and schedule performance. Examination of project results over time to determine whether performance is improving or deteriorating.

Triangulation Estimating - Triangulation estimating uses the premise that the most accurate estimate lies somewhere near the mean (average) of the most optimistic, most likely, and most pessimistic estimates.

User Requirements - Specific product, service, or other business need that the project is intended to meet.

Validation - Evaluation of a product against its specified requirements.

Validation Of Requirements - A review of requirements to confirm that the written definition clearly defines the intended use. Answers the question: Are we building the right product?

Variable Cost - Unit of cost that varies with production quantity, such as material or direct labor required to complete a product or project.

Unmanageable Risk - Risk for which it is impossible to reduce the likelihood of occurrence or amount at stake.

Update - Revision reflecting the most current information on the project.

Useful Life - Amount of time during which a product will provide a return or value to its owner or user.

User - Ultimate customer for the product; the people who will actually use it.

Vendor - Distributors of commonly available goods or services when requirements and specifications are well defined.

Verifiable Requirement - A requirement stated in measurable terms and quantified in a manner that can be determined by inspection, analysis, demonstration, or testing.

Verification of Requirements - A review of work products to ensure that they meet the specified requirements. Answers the question: are we building the product right?

Virtual Team - Project team that is not physically co-located and whose interaction occurs primarily through electronic networks such as the internet, intranet, or other configurations to ensure a team environment is established and maintained.

Variance - Actual or potential deviation from an intended or budgeted amount or plan. Difference between a plan and actual time, cost, or performance.

Variance Analysis - Comparison of actual project results to planned or expected results.

Variance At Completion (VAC) - In the earned value method, the difference between the BAC and the EAC (VAC=BAC-EAC).

Variance Threshold - Predetermined cost, schedule, or performance parameter that, when realized causes an action. For example, the project's cost-schedule

Copyright © Mometrix Media. You have been licensed one copy of this document for personal use only. Any other reproduction or redistribution is strictly prohibited. All rights reserved.

variance threshold may be set at 20%, so that any variance greater than 20% would require an action, such as reporting the even to senior management, holding a project review, or redefining the project's scope.

WBS Dictionary - Collection of work package descriptions that includes, among other things, planning information such as schedule dates, cost budgets, and staff assignments. WBS index of WBS elements set up by indenture.

Weak Matrix - Organizational structure in which the balance of power over project resources shifts in the direction of the functional manager, and the project manager has less decision-making influence and authority.

What-If Analysis - Process of evaluating alternative strategies, by changing certain variables and assumptions to predict the outcome of considering such changes.

Waiver - Intentional or voluntary relinquishment of a known right or conduct that warrants an inference that the right has been relinquished. Under the doctrine of waiver, a party can relinquish rights he or she has under the contract. For example, the right to strict performance is waived if the contractor delivers incomplete or defective products or delivers after the scheduled date and the project manager does not object or demand that the defects be corrected.

Walk-through - A peer review and examination of the requirements, design or implementation of a project by qualified experts to ensure that the project objectives will be met. Process used by software developers whereby a group of knowledgeable peers mentally step through the design and logic flow of a program with test cases to identify errors and inconsistencies. Rehearsal of an operational procedure by stimulating the execution of all its steps except those that are high risk or prohibitively expensive.

WBS (Work Breakdown Structure) - A deliverable-oriented grouping of project elements, which organizes and defines the total scope of the project. Each descending level provides a more detailed description of a project element. It is the definition of the work scope.

Work Product - Any artifact created as part of defining, maintaining, or using a software process, including process descriptions, plans, procedures, computer programs, and associated documentation, which may or may not be intended for delivery to a customer or end user. Any final or intermediate product, service or result of a process or activity.

Win-Lose - Outcome of conflict resolution that typically makes use of the power available to each party and treats conflict as a zero-sum game.

Win-Win - Outcome of conflict resolution that results in both parties being better off. Focuses on the objectives of both parties and the ways to meet those objectives while resolving the issue at hand.

Work Acceptance - Work is considered accepted when it is conducted, documented, and verified according to acceptance criteria provided in the technical specifications and contract documents.

Work Authorization - Permission for specific work to be performed during a

Copyright © Mometrix Media. You have been licensed one copy of this document for personal use only. Any other reproduction or redistribution is strictly prohibited. All rights reserved.

specific period; generally used in cases where work is to be performed in segments because of technical or funding limitations.

Zero Defect (ZD) - Quality standard, first articulated by Philip Crosby that asserts that nothing less than 100 percent quality should be the goal of an organization.

Zero Variance - Situation in which the planned date or cost is equal to the actual date or cost of any activity or project. This is a rare event in most projects.

Acronyms

AGA - Association of Government Auditors

AIMS - Agency Information Management Strategy

ANSI - American National Standards Institute

APD - Advance Planning Document

APDU - Advance Planning Document Update

ARM - Acquisition Risk Management

ASAP - As Soon As Possible

ASCII - American Standard Code for Information Interchange

ATP - Acceptance Test Plan

BCC - Blind Carbon Copy

BCC - Budget Change Concept

BCP - Budget Change Proposal

BL - Budget Letter

BP - Best Practices

BPSG - Best Practices Support Group

CAP - Corrective Action Plan

CAP - Cost Account/Allocation Plan

CBT - Computer Based Training

CC - Carbon Copy

CCP - Change Control Process

CFR - Code of Federal Regulations

CIO - Chief Information Officer

CLIN - Contract Line Item Number

CMIPS - Case Management Information and Payrolling System

ConOp - Concept of Operations document

COTS - Commercial Off The Shelf

CPAF - Cost Plus Award Fee

CPFF - Cost Plus Fixed Fee

CPIF - Cost Plus Incentive Fee

CPM - Contract Performance Management (CMM)

CPU - Central Processing Unit

CR - Cost Reimbursable

CS - Cost-Sharing

CTO - Contract Tracking and Oversight (CMM)

DB - Database

DBDD - Database Design Description

DBMS - Database Management System

DD - Database Design

DD - Design Document

DDE - Deliverable Document Evaluation

DED - Deliverable Expectation Document

DID - Data Item Description

DSD - Detailed Systems Design

EAW - Economic Analysis Worksheet/Workbook

EBT - Electronic Benefit Transfer

ECP - Engineering Change Proposal

EDI - Electronic Data Interchange

EDP - Electronic Data Processing

EFT - Electronic Funds Transfer

EIA - Electronic Industries Alliance

FAQ - Frequently Asked Questions

FFP - Firm Fixed Price

FFPLOE - Firm Fixed Price Level of Effort Contract

FG - Focus Group

FM - Functional Manager

FP - Fixed Price

FP - Function Point

FPAF - Fixed Price Award Fee

Copyright © Mometrix Media. You have been licensed one copy of this document for personal use only. Any other reproduction or redistribution is strictly prohibited. All rights reserved.

FPIF - Fixed Price Incentive Fee

FPIS - Fixed Price Incentive with Successive Targets

FPRP - Fixed Price Contract with Prospective Price

FPRR - Fixed Ceiling Price Contract with Retroactive Price

FSR - Feasibility Study Report

FY - Fiscal Year

GSD - General Systems Design

H/W - Hardware

HD - Help Desk

HTML - Hyper Text Markup Language

HW - Hardware

IA - Inter-Agency Agreement

IAA - Inter-Agency Agreement

IAPD/U - Implementation Advanced Planning Document/Update

ICD - Interface Control Document

ICWG - Interface Control Working Group

IDD - Interface Design Document

IDEF - Integration Definition (design modeling)

IFB - Invitation for Bid

IRD - Interface Requirements Document

IT - Information Technology

ITP - Invitation to Partner

ITPP - Information Technology Procurement Plan

JAD - Joint Application Design

LAN - Local Area Network

LD - Liquidated Damage(s)

LH - Labor Hour

LL - Lessons Learned

LOC - Lines of Code

LOE - Level of Effort

M&O - Maintenance and Operations

MAC - Move, Add, and/or Change

MM - Management Memo

MOTS - Modified Off The Shelf

MOU - Memorandum of Understanding

MPP - Master Project Plan

MQ - Minimum Qualifications

MSA - Master Services Agreement

MSC - Management Steering Council

MTS - Management Tracking System (tool)

N/A - Not Applicable

NLT - No Later Than

NOA - Notice of Action

OE&E - Operating Expenses and Equipment

OJT - On-the-Job-Training

OPR - Office of Primary Responsibility

PAPD/U - Planning Advance Planning Document/Update

PAT - Process Action Team

PD - Position Description

PDA - Personal Digital Assistant (such as Palm, Handspring, etc.)

PDF - Adobe's Portable Document Format

PDM - Process Definition and Maintenance (CMM)

PE - Planning Estimate

PIER - Post Implementation Evaluation Report

PMI - Project Management Institute

PMM - Project Management Methodology

PMO - Project Management Office

PO - Project Office

PO - Purchase Order

POC - Point of Contact

POST - Project Office Support Tool(s)

PPM - Project Performance Management (CMM)

PSM - Practical Software Measurement

PY - Personnel Year

QA - Quality Assurance

QAP - Quality Assurance Plan

QAWG - Quality Assurance Working Group

R&D - Research and Development

Copyright © Mometrix Media. You have been licensed one copy of this document for personal use only. Any other reproduction or redistribution is strictly prohibited. All rights reserved.

R&R - Roles and Responsibilities

RAM - Responsibility Assignment Matrix

RAM - Risk Assessment Model

RDM - Requirements Development and Management

RFI - Request for Interest

RFP - Request For Proposal

RMP - Risk Management Plan

S/W - Software

SAP - Software Acquisition Planning

SD - Systems Development

SDD - Software Design Document

SDF - Software Development File

SDLC - Software Development Life Cycle

SDP - Software Development Plan

SE - Software Engineering

SI - System Implementation

SIDD - System Interface Design Document

SLA - Service Level Agreement

SLOC - Source Line of Code

SME - Subject Matter Expert

SOL - Solicitation

SOP - Standard Operating Procedure

SOW - Statement Of Work

SPOC - Single Point of Contact

SPR - Special Project Report

SQAP - Software Quality Assurance Plan

SQL - Structured Query Language

SRE - Software Risk Evaluation

SRS - Software Requirements Specification

STP - Software Test Plan

STR - Software Test Report

T&C - Terms and Conditions

T&E - Test and Evaluation

T&M - Time and Materials

TBD - To Be Determined

TOC - Table of Contents

TP - Training Program

TTS - Transition To Support

UT - Unit Test

V&V - Verification and Validation

VDD - Version Description Document

WAN - Wide Area Network

WBS - Work Breakdown Structure

WO - Work Order

ZD - Unit of cost that varies with production quantity, such as material or direct labor required to complete a product or project.

Formulas

Straight Line Depreciation - Cost-Salvage/Time

Double Declining Balance - Double the SL Depreciation; $ X original cost - accumulated depreciation

Sum of Years (SOY) - (Cost-Salvage) X year/sum of years (3-2-1/6)

Copyright © Mometrix Media. You have been licensed one copy of this document for personal use only. Any other reproduction or redistribution is strictly prohibited. All rights reserved.

Practice Test

Practice Questions

1. Effective project managers typically share three characteristics:
    a. Knowledge, performance, and strong personal effectiveness
    b. Risk taking, flexibility, and team leadership
    c. Knowledge, strong management skills, and organization.
    d. Leadership skills, cost effectiveness, and organization

2. Cost benefit analysis and selection criteria are:
    a. Part of an organization's internal processes
    b. Decision-making techniques
    c. Project selection methods
    d. Procedures that need approval

3. When is a project officially authorized?
    a. When all the stakeholders have been identified
    b. When the project budget has been approved
    c. When customer needs and expectations have been documented
    d. When the project charter has been approved

4. Project initiating processes should begin:
    a. In the initiating process stage only
    b. During the planning stage of the project
    c. During the execution stage of the project
    d. At the beginning of each phase

5. Project approval and funding are handled:
    a. When the project team documents the project charter
    b. By the major stakeholders
    c. External to the project boundaries
    d. At each stage of the project processes

6. A project statement of work (SOW) contains a:
    a. Project budget, charter, and strategic plan
    b. Project scope description, budget, and strategic plan
    c. Business plan, product scope description, and strategic plan
    d. Business case, charter, and product scope description

Copyright © Mometrix Media. You have been licensed one copy of this document for personal use only. Any other reproduction or redistribution is strictly prohibited. All rights reserved.

7. A business case usually contains the:
    a. Strategic plan and the organizational need
    b. Business need and the cost-benefit analysis
    c. Product scope description and the cost-benefit analysis
    d. Organizational need and the business need

8. A detailed description of a project or process to be delivered is called a:
    a. Business plan
    b. Case analysis
    c. Project scope
    d. Plan analysis

9. Project stakeholders are:
    a. External audiences such as the news media
    b. Employees within the organization
    c. Persons and audiences, both internal and external, who are involved in the project or
       process, who may affect the outcome of the project
    d. executive decision makers only

10. Identifying and prioritizing risks by their probability of occurrence and affect on a
project or process is a:
    a. Quantitative risk analysis
    b Risk action plan
    c. Risk management plan
    d. Qualitative risk analysis

11. In order to understand a project and its limitations, project managers must know:
    a. Risk identification and estimation tools and techniques, historical information, and
       current skills available in the internal organization
    b. Customer needs and available budget
    c. Customer organizational structure, risk identification and estimation tools and
       techniques, and customer internal goals
    d. Project objectives, interview techniques, and organizational structure, policies, and
       procedures

12. In order to obtain project approval, client commitment, and project acceptance, project
managers need skills in:
    a. Facilitating skills, active listening, and documenting abilities
    b. Negotiating, role-playing, and building consensus
    c. Communicating, preparing a presentation, and presenting the project vision that
       convinces an audience
    d. Communicating, facilitating, and interview techniques

13. During the project planning phase the processes performed are:
    a. Developing the project management plan and the project documents
    b. Setting up project tracking tools and project templates
    c. Status reporting and time management
    d. Identification of risks and plan risk responses

*Copyright © Mometrix Media. You have been licensed one copy of this document for personal use only.
Any other reproduction or redistribution is strictly prohibited. All rights reserved.*

14. Continual detailing of the project management plan is often called:
   a. Project life cycle
   b. Project charter
   c. Rolling wave planning
   d. Ongoing processes

15. Requirement-gathering techniques include:
   a. Planning sessions, focus groups, and brainstorming sessions
   b. Project schedule updates and scope changes
   c. Requirement collecting
   d. Identifying risks and risk responses

16. The primary source of information for the planning, execution, monitoring, and controlling and closing of a project is the:
   a. Project charter
   b. Work breakdown structure
   c. Project management plan
   d. Project scope

17. The process of subdividing project deliverables and work into small components is called the:
   a. Project scope
   b. Work breakdown structure
   c. Requirements documentation
   d. Project management plan

18. Collect requirements is:
   a. A detailed description of the project
   b. The process of defining and documenting stakeholder needs to meet project objectives
   c. The stakeholder register
   d. The work breakdown structure

19. A configuration management system provides:
   a. New or revised cost estimates
   b. A uniform and efficient way to centrally manage approved project changes
   c. A configuration verification audit
   d. A flowchart of team members

20. Defining team roles and responsibilities to create a project organization structure helps:
   a. Identify key project team members
   b. Build a communication plan
   c. Helps finalize the organizational structure
   d. Identify project deliverables

Copyright © Mometrix Media. You have been licensed one copy of this document for personal use only. Any other reproduction or redistribution is strictly prohibited. All rights reserved.

21. Sequence activities are:
 a. The specific actions that produce a project's deliverables
 b. An estimate of the materials needed to perform a project's deliverables
 c. The process of identifying and documenting the relationships of the project's activities
 d. Activity sequences, resource requirements, and schedule constraints

22. Estimate activity resources is:
 a. The process of estimating the type and quantities of material, equipment, or supplies needed to perform each project activity
 b. The process of estimating the number of work periods needed to complete individual activities with resources
 c. The actions needed to produce deliverables
 d. The resource requirements and schedule constraints

23. The process of approximating the number of work periods needed to complete individual activities with estimate resources is:
 a. Sequence activity
 b. A schedule
 c. Estimate activity duration
 d. An output

24. Analyzing activity sequences, durations, resource requirements, and schedule constraints in order to create a project schedule is called:
 a. Estimate activity resources
 b. Develop schedule
 c. Output
 d. Defined activity

25. Developing an approximation of the money needed to complete a project is a:
 a. Scope baseline
 b. Risk register
 c. Cost estimate
 d. Activity

26. The estimated costs of individual activities that establish an authorized cost baseline is a:
 a. Cost estimate.
 b. Budget
 c. An estimated output
 d. Scope baseline

27. The outputs of a determined budget include:
 a. Activity cost estimate, scope baseline, and project document updates
 b. Cost performance baseline, document update, and basis of estimates
 c. Basis of estimates, resources, and project funding requirements
 d. Cost performance baseline, project funding requirements, and project document updates

Copyright © Mometrix Media. You have been licensed one copy of this document for personal use only. Any other reproduction or redistribution is strictly prohibited. All rights reserved.

28. The identification and documentation of project roles, responsibilities required skills, reporting relationships, and a staffing management plan is a:
    a. Plan communication
    b. Human resource plan
    c. Quality requirement
    d. Risk management plan

29. Defining how to conduct risk management activities for a project is called a:
    a. Plan risk management
    b. Communication plan
    c. Quality plan
    d. Environmental factor

30. Defining how changes will be handled in order to manage risks requires a knowledge of:
    a. Scope, project deliverables, project requirements, configuration management, and the change management plan
    b. Negotiating, documenting, and project dissemination
    c. Project deliverables and requirements and the risk management plan
    d. Scope, change management plan, and the plan procurement

31. The process of putting together options and actions to enhance opportunities and reduce threats is called:
    a. A risks register
    b. A risk analysis
    c. A communication plan
    d. A plan risk response

32. Documenting project decisions, specifying the project approach, and identifying potential sellers is called:
    a. A marketing plan
    b. A plan procurement
    c. A scope plan
    d. Communication plan

33. The processes performed to complete the work in the project management plan, according to specifications is called:
    a. The executing process group
    b. A scope plan
    c. A process plan
    d. A contract

34. To gain project plan approval from the customer and to formalize the management approach, project managers should have a knowledge of:
    a. The project charter, the project plan, and the stakeholders' expectations
    b. Forecasting, the project charter, and the stakeholders' expectations
    c. Stakeholder' expectations, acceptance criteria, and the organizational structure, plan, and procedures
    d. Negotiating, presenting, and influencing the stakeholders

Copyright © Mometrix Media. You have been licensed one copy of this document for personal use only. Any other reproduction or redistribution is strictly prohibited. All rights reserved.

35. Improving team competencies, team interaction, and the team environment to enhance a project's performance is called:
  a. Monitoring the process
  b. Managing the stockholder's expectations
  c. Distributing information
  d. Developing a project team

36. When meeting with key stakeholders to begin a project, a project manager should:
  a. Have skills in presenting and motivating
  b. Be good at disseminating information and collating
  c. Have knowledge of the risk mitigation techniques
  d. Use scheduling tools

37. In order to complete the project tasks and achieve the project goals, a project manager must know:
  a. The project plan and effective ways to measurement the outcomes
  b. How to direct and manage the project actions
  c. Company procedures and policies
  d. The project plan, statement of work, configuration management, and company procedures and policies

38. During the project execution, some results may require the project manager to make changes including:
  a. The project charter
  b. Activity durations, resource productivity, and unanticipated risks
  c. Customer organizational structure and resource productivity
  d. Reinitiating the project

39. A large portion of a project's budget is used during:
  a. The planning stage
  b. The execution stage
  c. Monitoring and controlling the project
  d. The initial stage of the project

40. Some outputs of managing and directing a project are:
  a. Enterprise environmental factors and the project management plan
  b. Approved change requests and project document updates
  c. Change requests and the project management plan
  d. Deliverables, work performance information, change requests, project management plan updates, and project document updates

41. The process of auditing quality needs and results from quality control measurements is:
  a. An executing process
  b. A baseline audit
  C. Perform quality assurance
  D. An organizational process

Copyright © Mometrix Media. You have been licensed one copy of this document for personal use only. Any other reproduction or redistribution is strictly prohibited. All rights reserved.

42. Obtaining seller responses, selecting seller responses, and awarding contracts is called:
    a. Make-or-buy agreements
    b. Teaming agreements
    c. Conduct procurements
    d. Source selection criteria

43. The process of communicating and working with stakeholders to meet their needs is called:
    a. Managing stakeholder expectations
    b. Quality assurance
    c. Managing project expectations
    d. Project document updates

44. Project managers should set expectations in accordance with the project plan because:
    a. It helps stakeholders understand the contract administration
    b. It meets stakeholders' interests and helps them understand the plan limitations
    c. It helps align the stakeholders and the team members
    d. It helps team members negotiate the terms of the project plan

45. Documents used in bid and proposal activities, including request for information, request for quotations, and the buyer's invitation for bid are called:
    a. Output/Inputs
    b. Procurement documents
    c. Procurement management plans
    d. Portfolios

46. Plan procurements identify:
    a. Project needs that can be best met by acquiring products, services outside the organization versus those needs best accomplished by the project team
    b. The requirements of the project
    c. Teaming agreements
    d. Risk considerations, inputs, and tools and techniques

47. Some tools and techniques used during procurement management include:
    a. Risk registers, expert judgment, and baseline cost performance
    b. Contract types, risk registers, and baseline cost performance
    c. Make-or-buy analysis, expert judgment, and contract types
    d. Make-or-buy analysis, project schedule, and risk registers

48. Each selected seller in a contract receives a:
    a. Performance report
    b. Schedule
    c. Procurement contract
    d. Budget and time constraint schedule

Copyright © Mometrix Media. You have been licensed one copy of this document for personal use only. Any other reproduction or redistribution is strictly prohibited. All rights reserved.

49. Implementing the procurement of project resources that align with the procurement plan requires skills in:
   a. Negotiating and analyzing
   b. Presenting and leading
   c. Facilitating and coordinating
   d. Negotiating and coordinating

50. The quality management plan describes:
   a. Requirements of the project plan
   b. How the project management team will put into action the performing organization's quality policy
   c. The report performance
   d. Cost/schedule risks

51. The quality management plan is a subsidiary plan of the:
   a. Project scope
   b. Project schedule
   c. Performance report
   d. Project management plan

52. Approved change requests often require:
   a. Baseline revisions and cost changes
   b. New or revised cost estimates, activity sequences, schedule dates, and resource requirements
   c. New or revised cost estimates, resource requirements, and updated automated systems
   d. Cost changes and configuration management

53. Participants in risk identification activities should include:
   a. The project manager only
   b. Select members of the project team
   c. Subject matter experts
   d. All project personnel

54. Some tools and techniques involved in identifying risks include:
   a. Risk management plan, environmental factors, and the risk register
   b. Project documents and activity cost estimates
   c. Risk management plan, activity cost estimates, and SWOT analysis
   d. Documentation reviews, checklist analysis, SWOT analysis, and assumptions analysis

55. The output of risk identification is:
   a. Assumptions analysis
   b. Expert judgment
   c. Checklist analysis
   d. Risk register

Copyright © Mometrix Media. You have been licensed one copy of this document for personal use only. Any other reproduction or redistribution is strictly prohibited. All rights reserved.

56. The Delphi technique, an information gathering technique, is:
    a. A way to reach of consensus of experts
    b. A diagram technique
    c. Review structure
    d. A root cause analysis

57. Two quantitative risk analysis tools used to gather data are:
    a. Expert judgments and interviewing
    b. Probability distributions and cost estimates
    c. Interviewing and probability distributions
    d. Probability matrix and Impact matrix

58. The process of implementing risk response plans, tracking identified risks, monitoring and identifying new risks, and evaluating risk process effectiveness is:
    a. Monitor and control risks
    b. A risks register
    c. Work performance information
    d. Technical performance measurement

59. The performance of a successful team is measured:
    a. Through the organization's viewpoint
    b. Through technical success according to agreed-upon project objectives, project schedule, performance, and budget performance
    c. Through a reduced staff turnover rate
    d. Through the feedback of all team members

60. Team management involves a combination of skills with an emphasis on:
    a. Frequent team meetings
    b. Conflict management and team reviews
    c. Communication, conflict management, negotiation, and leadership
    d. team training

61. As a result of managing a project, the project manager:
    a. Submits change requests, updates the HR plan, resolves issues, provides performance appraisals, and records lessons learned
    b. Provides team organization reports, resolves issues, and provides feedback to the key stakeholders
    c. Recognizes roles and responsibilities, updates the staffing management plan, and re-assigns team roles as needed
    d. Updates templates according to lesson-learned documentation, organizes standard processes, and reports all actions to the organization

62. High-performance teams are characterized by:
    a. Individual behavior and team efficiency
    b. Training, coaching and mentoring from the project manager
    c. Task-oriented and results-oriented outcomes
    d. Individual performance of each team member

Copyright © Mometrix Media. You have been licensed one copy of this document for personal use only. Any other reproduction or redistribution is strictly prohibited. All rights reserved.

63. The success of project managers in managing their project teams often depends upon:
    a. Their ability to encourage team members
    b. Their one-on-one interaction with all team members
    c. Their ability to resolve conflicts
    d. Their attitude towards team members

64. Processes necessary to track, review, and regulate the progress and performance of the project are:
    a. Communication efforts
    b. Quality assurance performances
    c. Management of project inputs and outputs
    d. Monitoring and controlling processes

65. The key benefit of monitoring and controlling is:
    a. Project performance is observed and measured regularly and consistently
    b. Manage stakeholder expectations
    c. Keep team members apprised of process activities
    d. Keep procurements up-to-date

66. Common formats for performance reports include:
    a. Charts, employee evaluations, and reporting systems
    b. Change requests, histograms, and employee evaluations
    c. Bar charts, S-curves, histograms, and tables
    d. Change requests, reporting systems, team evaluations, and variance analysis

67. Monitoring includes:
    a. Status reporting, progress measurement, and forecasting
    b. Requirements documentation, change requests, and environmental factors
    c. Forecasting, organizational updates, and change control processes
    d. Traceability matrixes, progress measurements, and organizational updates

68. Control costs is the process of:
    a. Collecting and distributing performance information including status reports, progress measurements, and forecasts
    b. Monitoring and recording results to assess performance and recommend necessary changes
    c. Monitoring the status of the project to update the project budget and manage changes to the cost baseline
    d. Implementing risk response plans, tracking identified risks, monitoring residual risks, and evaluating risk progress effectiveness

69. Examining project performance over time to determine if a performance is improving or deteriorating is a:
    a. Earned value performance
    b. Variance analysis
    c. Trend analysis
    d. Performance index

Copyright © Mometrix Media. You have been licensed one copy of this document for personal use only. Any other reproduction or redistribution is strictly prohibited. All rights reserved.

70. The process of comparing actual project performance to planned or expected performance is:
    a. Trend analysis
    b. Variance analysis
    c. Work performance measurements
    d. Budget forecasts

71. The process of reviewing all change requests, approving changes, and managing changes to deliverables and other documents is:
    a. Integrated change control process
    b. Scope verification
    c. Performance change reports
    d. Monitoring possible risks

72. Performance reports provide information on a project's performance through:
    a. Inputs and outputs
    b. Updates to the project plan
    c. Scope, schedule, cost, resources, quality, and risk
    d. Cost, trends, risk analysis, and document updates

73. The process of formalizing acceptance of completed project deliverables is:
    a. Project plan management
    b. Verify scope
    c. Status reporting
    d. Performance measuring

74. The process of monitoring and recording results of quality activities to assess performance and recommend needed changes is:
    a. Report performance
    b. Control scope
    c. Work performance
    d. Perform quality control

75. Some outputs of a report performance include:
    a. Quality control measurements, change requests, and project document updates
    b. Project document updates and risk register updates
    c. Budget forecast, change requests, and project management plan updates
    d. Performance reports, organizational process assets updates, and change requests

76. Some tools and techniques used to ensure project results conform to quality standards include:
    a. Reporting procedures, flow charts, and project templates
    b. Inspection, matrixes, and project templates
    c. Testing, inspection, and control charts
    d. Interviews, process analysis, and testing

Copyright © Mometrix Media. You have been licensed one copy of this document for personal use only. Any other reproduction or redistribution is strictly prohibited. All rights reserved.

77. Examples of quality measurement tools are:
    a. Statistical sampling, control charts, flow-charts, and inspection
    b. Testing, interviews, and metrics
    c. Transference techniques, template comparisons, and mitigation
    d. Quality control measurements, work performance measurements, and sampling

78. Risk response techniques include:
    a. Facilitation planning and acceptance
    b. Transference, mitigation, insurance, and acceptance
    c. Brainstorming, inspection, and process analysis
    d. Identifying and analyzing issues and testing

79. The process of managing procurement relationships, monitoring contract performance, and making changes and corrections as needed is called:
    a. Administer procurements
    b. Close procurements
    c. Quality control
    d. Procurement analysis

80. Active listening helps project managers create a friendly atmosphere and helps them:
    a. Inspect and review team member's work
    b. Analyze issues to ensure corrective actions
    c. Get information from team members regarding work deviations
    d. Elaborate on project reports

81. Facilitation techniques help:
    a. Build consensus and overcome obstacles
    b. With feedback loops and barriers to communication
    c. Prepare an agenda and deal with conflicts
    d. Body language and visual aids design

82. Performance reports report key information such as:
    a. Budget updates and team reports
    b. Stakeholder risk tolerances, budget updates, and significant accomplishments
    c. Current status, significant accomplishments, scheduled activities, forecasts, and issues
    d. Significant accomplishments, forecasts, team evaluations, and financial controls

83. Developing options and actions to enhance opportunities and reduce threats is:
    a. Qualitative risk analysis
    b. Plan risk management
    c. Plan risk response
    d. Identifying risks

84. The Closing Process Group, when completed:
    a. Confirms that the defined project processes are completed and formally establishes the project is finished
    b. Completes all project procurements
    c. Evaluates risk response effectiveness throughout the project
    d. Evaluates the performance of the completed project

Copyright © Mometrix Media. You have been licensed one copy of this document for personal use only. Any other reproduction or redistribution is strictly prohibited. All rights reserved.

85. Two outputs of the close project phase are:
    a. Closed procurements and change requests
    b. Final project management updates and performance updates
    c. Work performance measurements and Organizational process asset updates
    d. Organizational process asset updates and final product or service result transition

86. At project close the project manager gains final acceptance from the customer by:
    a. Ensuring the delivered project complied with the agreed deliverables, agreed scope, and any organizational procedures
    b. Ensuring the delivered project complied with the original budget and project plan
    c. Signing a project complete contract and handing over all deliverables
    d. Handing over all completed policies and procedures

87. Some skills a project manager needs when formalizing final acceptance from the client include:
    a. Inspecting and reviewing, analyzing issues, and communicating
    b. Negotiating, communicating, and observation
    c. Negotiating, document writing, and managing conflict
    d. Motivating, presenting, and managing conflict

88. Having knowledge of budget, expenditure processing, and statutory requirements helps a project manager:
    a. Obtain financial, legal, and administrative closure for internal and external vendors and customers
    b. Complete the project within the customer's budget
    c. Ensure all project phases stayed within budget
    d. Finalize procurement completion

89. At project close project managers should communicate lessons learned through:
    a. Final project status to all stakeholders and post mortem team discussions
    b. Team discussions, 360-degree surveys, and supplier performance evaluations
    c. Industry best practice evaluations, appraisal of project scope, and definitions and performance metrics
    d. Stakeholder comments and team analysis

90. Project managers distribute final project reports in order to:
    a. Demonstrate the project methodology, show the customer organizational structure, and meet statutory requirements
    b. Project archives
    c. Highlight project variances, lessons learned, and final project status
    d. Show lessons learned and to comply with statutory requirements

91. Customer satisfaction can be measured at the project close through:
    a. Appropriate interview techniques and surveys
    b. Team feedback and project documents and records
    c. Statistical sampling and relationship building
    d. Industry best practices and surveys

Copyright © Mometrix Media. You have been licensed one copy of this document for personal use only. Any other reproduction or redistribution is strictly prohibited. All rights reserved.

92. Adhering to legal requirements, ethical standards, and social norms helps project managers:
    a. Keep their team members concentrated on their tasks
    b. Send updated reports to all stakeholders
    c. Ensure personal integrity and professionalism
    d. Ensure the integrity of the customer's organization

93. Skills that help ensure a personal integrity include:
    a. Communication and research techniques
    b. Personal strengths and risk analysis
    c. Sound judgment and research outputs
    d. Judgment and research of law and regulations and ethical standards

94. Project managers can help build the capabilities of their teams through a knowledge of:
    a. Effective communication techniques and organizational standards
    b. Project management body of knowledge and effective communication techniques
    c. Negotiation and transfer of knowledge
    d. Knowledge of legal requirements and organizational techniques

95. Project managers can improve their project management services through a knowledge of:
    a. Community values and legal requirements
    b. Tools and techniques
    c. Personal strengths and weaknesses and appropriate professional competencies
    d. Procurement expertise and judgment

96. Project managers can enhance their personal professional competence through skills including:
    a. Personal development and effective communication
    b. Knowing cultural differences and auditing practices
    c. Risks, assumptions, and communication
    d. Communication techniques and self-assessment strategies

97. Creating a healthy work environment requires skills in:
    a. Research techniques and documenting information
    b. Judgment calls and appropriate professional competencies
    c. Ethical standards and stakeholder values
    d. Resolving conflicts and effective communication

98. Project managers can help promote interaction among team members and other stakeholders in a professional manner by:
    a. Establishing an effective communications plan
    b. Motivating teams
    c. Respecting personal and cultural differences
    d. Planning personal development

Copyright © Mometrix Media. You have been licensed one copy of this document for personal use only. Any other reproduction or redistribution is strictly prohibited. All rights reserved.

99. Knowledge of interpersonal techniques and community and stakeholder values help:
   a. Establish a collaborative project management environment
   b. Ensure the personal integrity of team members
   c. Maintain communication between team members
   d. Team members plan personal development

100. Project managers can contribute to the project knowledge base by:
   a. Researching law and ethical standards
   b. Transferring project leadership to other team members
   c. Sharing lessons learned, best practices, and research
   d. Sharing corrective actions with team members

Copyright © Mometrix Media. You have been licensed one copy of this document for personal use only.
Any other reproduction or redistribution is strictly prohibited. All rights reserved.

Answers and explanations

1. A: When project managers combine their educational background and training with strong project accomplishments and personal traits, they usually succeed in their work. Project managers must select the right tools and techniques and management styles to fit each individual project.

2. C: Project managers meet with their clients and subject matter experts before they begin a new project in order to pair the best project methods to individual clients. Two examples of project selection methods are cost benefit analysis and selection criteria. Successful managers need to know the needs, expectations, business environment and internal goals of their client. They combine that with a personal knowledge of past projects, presentation techniques, and approval procedures.

3. D: New projects are defined in the initiating process group at the beginning of a project or process. During the initiating process period the project charter is determined by the initiator or sponsor of the project. The project charter is a formal document that gives the project manager the power to use the resources necessary to fulfill the project. Large projects may be separated into smaller phases to ensure the success of the project.

4. D: The project charter should be reviewed at the beginning of each phase of a project to ensure the project remains centered on the client's business need and objectives. When project team members and stakeholders are involved in all initiation processes, the project deliverables tend to be more successful and the clients more satisfied. Involved stakeholders are able to make informed decisions about the continuance and direction in all stages of a project.

5. C: Project approval and funding are not involved in the internal processes of the project. However, initial finances and funding are allocated in the beginning process stages so the project manager and other stakeholders can plan and begin the new project process. The project manager oversees the documentation of the project process, which includes the project scope, project outcomes, project timing, and a prediction of the financial resources needed from the organization.

6. C: A SOW is a story-like summary of a project's products or services that will be carried out in the project. An internal project, initiated by the project creator or sponsor, provides a work statement built on one of three variables: a business need, a product or service requirements. In external projects a SOW can be acquired from a customer as a bid project or can be acquired as part of a contract.

7. B: A business case contains information based on a business need and helps stakeholders determine if a project is feasible. The business case is initiated by one or more conditions including: market demand, customer request, organizational need, technological developments or legal necessities. A cost-benefit analysis is usually included in a business case. Projects with more than one phase might be analyzed on a regular basis in order to deliver the needed benefits.

Copyright © Mometrix Media. You have been licensed one copy of this document for personal use only. Any other reproduction or redistribution is strictly prohibited. All rights reserved.

8. C: A project and product scope both provide detailed descriptions of a future work to be done. A product scope gives specific characteristics or functions of a product, service or result. A project scope describes the necessary work to be carried out to provide a product, service, or result, along with the distinctive features and effects of the project. Project managers concentrate their focus on what defines and controls the project.

9. C: Stakeholders include people, both internal and external, who will work on or impact a project. Stakeholders should be identified at the beginning of a project and analyzed by their degree of involvement, their expectations, and rank of importance and influence. Successful strategies address the degree of importance each stakeholder has in the project and the timing of their involvement in the project. This analysis helps the project manger target those people most necessary to achieve project success.

10. D: A qualitative risk analysis determines a project's success through a focus on those risks most likely to happen, their impact, the necessary response timing, and other factors such as cost, scope, schedule, and quality. A qualitative risk analysis can be a fast and economical way to organize priorities for responses and can be a foundational step for a quantitative risk analysis or can lead straight to a project's plan risk responses.

11. A: Document reviews, the quality of the plans, and the consistency between plans and project requirements can identify risks in a project. Other informative techniques used in risk identification include brainstorming sessions, techniques to reach expert analysis, interviews of various audiences, checklists, expected scenarios, and risk diagramming methods. Historical information offers a good review, along with the available skills of the stakeholders. Root cause analysis helps identify obstacles and lead to corrective action.

12. C: Effective communication skills, successful presentation skills, and focused customer motivation are some of the necessary skills a project manager should possess in order to gain approval for projects. Decision makers are often convinced to pursue a project when the presenter delivers a powerful project vision or reason for a project. Effective storytelling is one method communicators often use to convince an audience. Prepared communicators know the organization's structure, policies, and procedures, along with the approval process before presenting to decision makers.

13. A: The project scope is defined, objectives are clarified, and a course of action is developed that will fulfill the project's objectives.

14. C: Rolling wave planning indicates consistent and regular planning and chronicling of project processes carried out.

15. A: Requirement-gathering techniques include planning meetings, role-playing, interviewing, consensus building, and active listening.

16. C: The project management plan is a chronicle of the activities that are essential to defining, integrating, and pulling together all secondary plans of a process or project. Some of the project inputs include the project charter, planning process outputs, enterprise environmental determinants, and organizational process benefits. The project management

Copyright © Mometrix Media. You have been licensed one copy of this document for personal use only. Any other reproduction or redistribution is strictly prohibited. All rights reserved.

plan is the authoritative document for the planning, executing, monitoring and controlling, and eventual closing of a project or process.

17. B: The create work breakdown structure (Create WBS) divides project deliverables and project work into smaller elements.

18. B: Collect requirements describe and document the necessary stakeholder needs for meeting a project's goals and purposes.

19. B: Configured managed systems with integrated change controls achieve several objectives in a project: They offer a progressive way to identify and apply changes in project standards, authenticate and advance projects, and provide a means of consistent communication of approved and rejected changes in a project.

20. A: Team member roles are based on their knowledge of the communication plan, the organizational structure, and stakeholder expectations.

21. C: Sequence activities identify and record the relationships between project actions with inputs including an activity list, activity attributes, a milestone list, a project scope statement, and the organization's process assets.

22. A: Some estimate activity process inputs include an activity list, activity attributes, resource calendars, organizational environment factors, and organizational process assets.

23. C: Estimate activity durations include inputs including an activity list, activity attributes, activity resource requirements, resource calendars, a project scope statement, organizational environmental factors, and process assets.

24. B: Develop schedule inputs include an activity list, activity attributes, activity resource requirements, project schedule network diagrams, resource calendars, and a project scope statement.

25. C: Cost estimate outputs include an activity cost estimate, a basis of estimates, and project document updates.

26. B: Budgets are approximated calculations of the cost of a project or scheduled activity.

27. D: Determined budgets calculate the anticipated costs of individual activities and help confirm a cost baseline.

28. B: Human resource plan inputs include activity resource requirements, enterprise environmental factors, and organizational process assets.

29. A: Plan risk management inputs include project scope statements, cost management plan, schedule management plans, and a communications management plan.

30. A: Project managers need negotiation skills, documentation, and dissemination in order to characterize how risks will be handled.

Copyright © Mometrix Media. You have been licensed one copy of this document for personal use only. Any other reproduction or redistribution is strictly prohibited. All rights reserved.

31. D: A plan risk response's outputs include risk register updates, risk-related contract decisions, project management plan updates, and project document updates.

32. B: Plan procurements outputs include procurement management plans, procurement statements of work, make-or-buy decisions, procurement documents, source selection criteria, and change requests.

33. A: Part of an executing process group includes matching people with resources and assimilating project activities that agree with the project management plan.

34. D: Project managers need skills in negotiation, presentation, and influence when meeting with clients to finalize a project management plan.

35. D: Develop project team inputs include project staff assignments, project management plans, and resource calendars. Outputs include team performance assessments and enterprise environmental updates.

36. A: Project managers need to know the project charter details, the project plan, and the organizational structure and have presentation and motivation skills.

37. D: When executing a project, managers need skills in leading and coordinating.

38. B: Project management analysis often requires modifications in the project plan and other documents.

39. B: Some of the executing management processes that entail part of the budget include quality assurance performance, the direction and management of the project and the development and management of the project team.

40. D: Inputs in the direction and management of a project include a project management plan, approved change requests, enterprise environmental factors, and organizational process assets.

41. C: Perform quality assurance helps guarantee the correct quality standards and operational definitions are used during the executing process stage.

42. C: Conduct procurement outputs are selected sellers, procurement contract awards, resource calendars, change requests, project management plan updates, and project document updates.

43. A: Managing stakeholder expectations includes a stakeholder register, stakeholder management strategy, a project management plan, an issue log, a change log, and organizational assets.

44. C: Some of the skills managers need to align stakeholder and team members are leading, facilitating, negotiating, and presenting.

45. B: Key project stakeholders, including suppliers, are involved in the procurement document process.

Copyright © Mometrix Media. You have been licensed one copy of this document for personal use only. Any other reproduction or redistribution is strictly prohibited. All rights reserved.

46. A: Identifying project needs that can be best met by acquiring products, services outside the organization versus those needs best accomplished by the project team is an important part of plan procurement.

47. C: Plan procurements impact the project schedule and strategy.

48. C: Some of the fundament elements a procurement award include: a statement of work, performance reporting, a schedule, roles and responsibilities, and pricing.

49. A: Project managers need to be familiar with cost estimation tools and techniques, contract administration, and organizational policies.

50. B: Customer satisfaction and prevention over inspection are prime considerations when designing a quality management plan.

51. D: Some of the tools and techniques in a quality plan include benchmarking, statistical sampling, flow charts, and other planning tools.

52. B: When change requests are altered it is often necessary to revise cost estimates, activity sequences, schedule dates, resource requirements, and risk response changes.

53. D: Some contributors in activities include the project manager, project team members, risk management team, customer, and end users.

54. D: Tools and techniques involved in identifying risks include documentation reviews, checklist analysis, and a SWOT analysis.

55. D: A risk register contains the qualitative risk analysis, a quantitative risk analysis, and a risk response planning document.

56. A: Subject experts are anonymous participants in the Delphi Technique.

57. C: Risk ranges and reasons are important parts of a risk interview.

58. A: Plan risks should be monitored continually during a project.

59. B: Project objectives are most likely met if teams effectively develop strategies and activities.

60. C: Project managers should continually challenge their team and reward them for outstanding performance.

61. A: Project managers should provide continual feedback and resolve issues when they arise.

62. C: Team success is calculated according the success of the agree-upon project objectives, timely delivery of outputs, and success of sticking to a budget.

Copyright © Mometrix Media. You have been licensed one copy of this document for personal use only. Any other reproduction or redistribution is strictly prohibited. All rights reserved.

63. C: Team conflict is natural and a team issue that is best resolved with the candidness of the team members.

64. D: Monitoring and controlling a process group requires that project performance be observed and measured in order to isolate any issues that might arise.

65. A: Monitoring and controlling processes includes: resolving problems, comparing project activities with the project management plan, and influencing factors that might disrupt the integrated change control.

66. C: Performance reports are distributed on a regular basis and can vary from a simple status updates to more complicated reports.

67. A: A project action on a performance report provides a project's performance with regard to scope observation, schedule, cost, resources, quality, and project risks.

68. C: Control cost inputs include information from the project management plan, project funding requirements, work performance information, and organizational process assets.

69. C: Other project performance reviews are variance analysis and earned value performance.

70. B: Performance reviews are safeguards that help ensure projects are on schedule and within the budget.

71. A: Outputs of an integrated change control process include change request status, project management plan updates, and project document updates.

72. C: Some outputs of monitoring and controlling project work include change requests, project management plan updates, and project document updates.

73. B: Outputs of the verify scope process include accepted deliverables, change requests, and project document updates.

74. D: Activities involved in the perform quality control process are quality control measurements, validated changes, validated deliverables, organizational process asset updates, change requests, project management plan updates, and project document updates.

75. D: The inputs of report performance include the project management plan, work performance information, work performance measurements, budget forecasts, and organizational process assets.
76. C: Project managers use differing tools and techniques to examine project deliverables in order to conform to customer requirements.

77. A: Project managers need knowledge of industry best practices and standards so they can provide customers with high quality work.

Copyright © Mometrix Media. You have been licensed one copy of this document for personal use only. Any other reproduction or redistribution is strictly prohibited. All rights reserved.

78. B: Other knowledge areas project managers should consider are risk management planning, brainstorming, facilitation techniques, and interview techniques.

79. A: Administer procurements outputs include procurement documentation, organizational process asset updates, change requests, and project management plan updates.

80. C: Active listening helps keep team members motivated and helps them gain ownership of their project responsibilities.

81. A: Some tools and techniques involved in facilitation techniques are communication methods and information distribution tools.

82. C: Activities, accomplishments, milestones, identified issues, and problems should be reported.

83. C: Project management processes are risk management planning, identification, analysis, response planning, and monitoring and controlling a project.

84. A: Some project phase closures include obtaining acceptance by the client, post-project review, documentation of lessons learned, and close out procurements.

85. D: Inputs of the close project phase include the project management plan, accepted deliverables, and organizational process assets.

86. A: Project managers need knowledge of the project scope, deliverables, acceptance criteria, organizational structure, and the statutory of the contract requirements.

87. C: Having knowledge of the project deliverables, acceptance criteria, policies and procedures, and legal aspects of the project are all necessary for project managers.

88. A: Other knowledge items that are helpful are conflict resolution and contract knowledge.

89. B: Communication, objectivity, analyzing, presenting, communicating, and facilitating are skills project managers need when closing a project.

90. C: Archiving project end documents requires skills in document writing and communicating.

91. A: Project managers should use their knowledge of a client's organizational structure and address the business need when finalizing a project.
92. C: Project integrity and professionalism are not only ethical, but also help protect a client's business interests.

93. D: Project managers need knowledge of legal requirements, ethical standards, social norms, community and stakeholder values, and communication techniques.

94. B: Lessons learned and best practices are critical to building a capable team.

Copyright © Mometrix Media. You have been licensed one copy of this document for personal use only. Any other reproduction or redistribution is strictly prohibited. All rights reserved.

95. C: Other knowledge skills project managers need include knowledge of instructional methods and tools, training, and self-assessment strategies.

96. A: Project managers need ongoing education and knowledge of laws to improve their professional skills.

97. D: Open communication and a knowledge of team members' strengths and weaknesses help create a healthy work environment.

98. C: Project managers with knowledge of interpersonal techniques, cultural differences, and team motivation strategies help promote positive interaction among their team members.

99. A: Cultural differences, communication techniques, and team motivation strategies are also helpful knowledge skills.

100. C: Documentation of lessons learned about project aspects and team members will help project managers on future projects.

Copyright © Mometrix Media. You have been licensed one copy of this document for personal use only. Any other reproduction or redistribution is strictly prohibited. All rights reserved.

Special Report: Which Study Guides and Practice Tests Are Worth Your Time

We believe the following practice tests and guide present uncommon value to our customers who wish to "really study" for the PMP tests. While our manual teaches some valuable tricks and tips that no one else covers, learning the basic coursework tested on the exam is also necessary.

Practice Tests

Official Practice Test Questions

http://www.pmi.org/info/PDC_PMPExamPreparation.asp

Request Assessment Form Link:

http://www.pmi.org/info/PDC_CertKnowAssess.asp

Study Guides

Project Management Certification for Dummies

http://www.booksamillion.com/ncom/books?id=3030450594057&pid=0764524518

Project Management Professional Certification Kit

http://www.booksamillion.com/ncom/books?id=3030450594057&pid=0782143253

These guides are THE best comprehensive coursework guides to the licensure exams. If you want to spend a couple months in preparation to squeeze every last drop out of your score, buy these books!

*Copyright © Mometrix Media. You have been licensed one copy of this document for personal use only.
Any other reproduction or redistribution is strictly prohibited. All rights reserved.*

Secret Key #1 – Time is Your Greatest Enemy

The table below shows the breakdown of the exam.
- Initiating the Project
- Planning the Project
- Executing the Project
- Controlling the Project
- Closing the Project
- Professional Responsibility

200 multiple choice questions – 4 hours on the computer
15 minute prep tutorial.

Success Strategy #1

Pace Yourself

Wear a watch to the PMP Test. At the beginning of the test, check the time (or start a chronometer on your watch to count the minutes), and check the time after each passage or every few questions to make sure you are "on schedule." For the computerized test an onscreen clock display will keep track of your remaining time, but it may be easier for you to monitor your pace based on how many minutes have been used, rather than how many minutes remain.

If you are forced to speed up, do it efficiently. Usually one or more answer choices can be eliminated without too much difficulty. Above all, don't panic. Don't speed up and just begin guessing at random choices. By pacing yourself, and continually monitoring your progress against the clock or your watch, you will always know exactly how far ahead or behind you are with your available time. If you find that you are one minute behind on the test, don't skip one question without spending any time on it, just to catch back up. Spend perhaps 45 seconds on the question and after four questions, you will have caught back up more gradually. Once you catch back up, you can continue working each problem at your normal pace.

Furthermore, don't dwell on the problems that you were rushed on. If a problem was taking up too much time and you made a hurried guess, it must be difficult. The difficult questions are the ones you are most likely to miss anyway, so it isn't a big loss. It is better to end with more time than you need than to run out of time. You can always go back and work the problems that you skipped. If you have time left over, as you review the skipped questions,

Copyright © Mometrix Media. You have been licensed one copy of this document for personal use only. Any other reproduction or redistribution is strictly prohibited. All rights reserved.

start at the earliest skipped question, spend at most another minute, and then move on to the next skipped question.

Lastly, sometimes it is beneficial to slow down if you are constantly getting ahead of time. You are always more likely to catch a careless mistake by working more slowly than quickly, and among very high-scoring test takers (those who are likely to have lots of time left over), careless errors affect the score more than mastery of material.

Secret Key #2 – Guessing is not Guesswork

You probably know that guessing is a good idea on the PMP test- unlike other standardized tests, there is no penalty for getting a wrong answer. Even if you have no idea about a question, you still have a 20-25% chance of getting it right.

Most test takers do not understand the impact that proper guessing can have on their score. Unless you score extremely high, guessing will significantly contribute to your final score.

Monkeys Take the PMP

What most test takers don't realize is that to insure that 20-25% chance, you have to guess randomly. If you put 20 monkeys in a room to take this test, assuming they answered once per question and behaved themselves, on average they would get 20-25% of the questions correct. Put 20 test takers in the room, and the average will be much lower among guessed questions. Why?

1. This test intentionally writes deceptive answer choices that "look" right. A test taker has no idea about a question, so picks the "best looking" answer, which is often wrong. The monkey has no idea what looks good and what doesn't, so will consistently be lucky about 20-25% of the time.
2. Test takers will eliminate answer choices from the guessing pool based on a hunch or intuition. Simple but correct answers often get excluded, leaving a 0% chance of being correct. The monkey has no clue, and often gets lucky with the best choice.

This is why the process of elimination endorsed by most test courses is flawed and detrimental to your performance- test takers don't guess, they make an ignorant stab in the dark that is usually worse than random.

Copyright © Mometrix Media. You have been licensed one copy of this document for personal use only. Any other reproduction or redistribution is strictly prohibited. All rights reserved.

Success Strategy #2

Let me introduce one of the most valuable ideas of this course- the $5 challenge:

You only mark your "best guess" if you are willing to bet $5 on it.
You only eliminate choices from guessing if you are willing to bet $5 on it.

Why $5? Five dollars is an amount of money that is small yet not insignificant, and can really add up fast (20 questions could cost you $100). Likewise, each answer choice on one question of the PMP will have a small impact on your overall score, but it can really add up to a lot of points in the end.

The process of elimination IS valuable. The following shows your chance of guessing it right:

If you eliminate this many choices:	Chance of getting it correct
0	20%
1	25%
2	33%
3	50%
4	100%

However, if you accidentally eliminate the right answer or go on a hunch for an incorrect answer, your chances drop dramatically: to 0%. By guessing among all the answer choices, you are GUARANTEED to have a shot at the right answer.

That's why the $5 test is so valuable- if you give up the advantage and safety of a pure guess, it had better be worth the risk.

What we still haven't covered is how to be sure that whatever guess you make is truly random. Here's the easiest way:

Always pick the first answer choice among those remaining.

Such a technique means that you have decided, **before you see a single test question**, exactly how you are going to guess- and since the order of choices tells you nothing about which one is correct, this guessing technique is perfectly random.

Copyright © Mometrix Media. You have been licensed one copy of this document for personal use only. Any other reproduction or redistribution is strictly prohibited. All rights reserved.

Secret Key #3 – Practice Smarter, Not Harder

Many test takers delay the test preparation process because they dread the awful amounts of practice time they think necessary to succeed on the test. We have refined an effective method that will take you only a fraction of the time.

There are a number of "obstacles" in your way on the PMP test. Among these are answering questions, finishing in time, and mastering test-taking strategies. All must be executed on the day of the test at peak performance, or your score will suffer. The PMP is a mental marathon that has a large impact on your future.

Just like a marathon runner, it is important to work your way up to the full challenge. So first you just worry about questions, and then time, and finally strategy:

Success Strategy

1. Find a good source for practice tests.
2. If you are willing to make a larger time investment, consider using more than one study guide- often the different approaches of multiple authors will help you "get" difficult concepts.
3. Take a practice test with no time constraints, with all study helps "open book." Take your time with questions and focus on applying strategies.
4. Take a practice test with time constraints, with all guides "open book."
5. Take a final practice test with no open material and time limits

If you have time to take more practice tests, just repeat step 5. By gradually exposing yourself to the full rigors of the test environment, you will condition your mind to the stress of test day and maximize your success.

Secret Key #4 - Prepare, Don't Procrastinate

Let me state an obvious fact: if you take the test three times, you will get three different scores. This is due to the way you feel on test day, the level of preparedness you have, and, despite the test writers' claims to the contrary, some tests WILL be easier for you than others.

Since your future depends so much on your score, you should maximize your chances of

Copyright © Mometrix Media. You have been licensed one copy of this document for personal use only. Any other reproduction or redistribution is strictly prohibited. All rights reserved.

success. In order to maximize the likelihood of success, you've got to prepare in advance. This means taking practice tests and spending time learning the information and test taking strategies you will need to succeed.

Never take the test as a "practice" test, expecting that you can just take it again if you need to. Feel free to take sample tests on your own, but when you go to take the official test, be prepared, be focused, and do your best the first time!

Secret Key #5 - Test Yourself

Everyone knows that time is money. There is no need to spend too much of your time or too little of your time preparing for the test. You should only spend as much of your precious time preparing as is necessary for you to get the score you need.

Once you have taken a practice test under real conditions of time constraints, then you will know if you are ready for the test or not.

If you have scored extremely high the first time that you take the practice test, then there is not much point in spending countless hours studying. You are already there.

Benchmark your abilities by retaking practice tests and seeing how much you have improved. Once you score high enough to guarantee success, then you are ready.

If you have scored well below where you need, then knuckle down and begin studying in earnest. Check your improvement regularly through the use of practice tests under real conditions. Above all, don't worry, panic, or give up. The key is perseverance!

Then, when you go to take the test, remain confident and remember how well you did on the practice tests. If you can score high enough on a practice test, then you can do the same on the real thing.

Copyright © Mometrix Media. You have been licensed one copy of this document for personal use only. Any other reproduction or redistribution is strictly prohibited. All rights reserved.

General Strategies

The most important thing you can do is to ignore your fears and jump into the test immediately- do not be overwhelmed by any strange-sounding terms. You have to jump into the test like jumping into a pool- all at once is the easiest way.

Make Predictions

As you read and understand the question, try to guess what the answer will be. Remember that several of the answer choices are wrong, and once you begin reading them, your mind will immediately become cluttered with answer choices designed to throw you off. Your mind is typically the most focused immediately after you have read the question and digested its contents. If you can, try to predict what the correct answer will be. You may be surprised at what you can predict.

Quickly scan the choices and see if your prediction is in the listed answer choices. If it is, then you can be quite confident that you have the right answer. It still won't hurt to check the other answer choices, but most of the time, you've got it!

Answer the Question

It may seem obvious to only pick answer choices that answer the question, but the test writers can create some excellent answer choices that are wrong. Don't pick an answer just because it sounds right, or you believe it to be true. It MUST answer the question. Once you've made your selection, always go back and check it against the question and make sure that you didn't misread the question, and the answer choice does answer the question posed.

Benchmark

After you read the first answer choice, decide if you think it sounds correct or not. If it doesn't, move on to the next answer choice. If it does, mentally mark that answer choice. This doesn't mean that you've definitely selected it as your answer choice, it just means that it's the best you've seen thus far. Go ahead and read the next choice. If the next choice is worse than the one you've already selected, keep going to the next answer choice. If the next choice is better than the choice you've already selected, mentally mark the new answer choice as your best guess.

The first answer choice that you select becomes your standard. Every other answer choice must be benchmarked against that standard. That choice is correct until proven otherwise by another answer choice beating it out. Once you've decided that no other answer choice seems as good, do one final check to ensure that your answer choice answers the question posed.

Valid Information

Don't discount any of the information provided in the question. Every piece of information may be necessary to determine the correct answer. None of the information in the question is there to throw you off (while the answer choices will certainly have information to throw you off). If two seemingly unrelated topics are discussed, don't ignore either. You can be confident there is a relationship, or it wouldn't be included in the question, and you are probably going to have to determine what is that relationship to find the answer.

Avoid "Fact Traps"

Don't get distracted by a choice that is factually true. Your search is for the answer that answers the question. Stay focused and don't fall for an answer that is true but incorrect. Always go back to the question and make sure you're choosing an answer that actually answers the question and is not just a true statement. An answer can be factually correct, but it MUST answer the question asked. Additionally, two answers can both be seemingly correct, so be sure to read all of the answer choices, and make sure that you get the one that BEST answers the question.

Milk the Question

Some of the questions may throw you completely off. They might deal with a subject you have not been exposed to, or one that you haven't reviewed in years. While your lack of knowledge about the subject will be a hindrance, the question itself can give you many clues that will help you find the correct answer. Read the question carefully and look for clues. Watch particularly for adjectives and nouns describing difficult terms or words that you don't recognize. Regardless of if you completely understand a word or not, replacing it with a synonym either provided or one you more familiar with may help you to understand what the questions are asking. Rather than wracking your mind about specific detailed information concerning a difficult term or word, try to use mental substitutes that are easier to understand.

The Trap of Familiarity

Don't just choose a word because you recognize it. On difficult questions, you may not recognize a number of words in the answer choices. The test writers don't put "make-believe" words on the test; so don't think that just because you only recognize all the words in one answer choice means that answer choice must be correct. If you only recognize words in one answer choice, then focus on that one. Is it correct? Try your best to determine if it is correct. If it is, that is great, but if it doesn't, eliminate it. Each word and answer choice you eliminate increases your chances of getting the question correct, even if you then have to guess among the unfamiliar choices.

Eliminate Answers

Eliminate choices as soon as you realize they are wrong. But be careful! Make sure you consider all of the possible answer choices. Just because one appears right, doesn't mean that the next one won't be even better! The test writers will usually put more than one good answer choice for every question, so read all of them. Don't worry if you are stuck between two that seem right. By getting down to just two remaining possible choices, your odds are now 50/50. Rather than wasting too much time, play the odds. You are guessing, but guessing wisely, because you've been able to knock out some of the answer choices that you know are wrong. If you are eliminating choices and realize that the last answer choice you are left with is also obviously wrong, don't panic. Start over and consider each choice again. There may easily be something that you missed the first time and will realize on the second pass.

Tough Questions

If you are stumped on a problem or it appears too hard or too difficult, don't waste time. Move on! Remember though, if you can quickly check for obviously incorrect answer choices, your chances of guessing correctly are greatly improved. Before you completely give up, at least try to knock out a couple of possible answers. Eliminate what you can and then guess at the remaining answer choices before moving on.

Brainstorm

If you get stuck on a difficult question, spend a few seconds quickly brainstorming. Run through the complete list of possible answer choices. Look at each choice and ask yourself, "Could this answer the question satisfactorily?" Go through each answer choice and consider it independently of the other. By systematically going through all possibilities, you may find something that you would otherwise overlook. Remember that when you get stuck, it's important to try to keep moving.

Read Carefully

Understand the problem. Read the question and answer choices carefully. Don't miss the question because you misread the terms. You have plenty of time to read each question thoroughly and make sure you understand what is being asked. Yet a happy medium must be attained, so don't waste too much time. You must read carefully, but efficiently.

Face Value

When in doubt, use common sense. Always accept the situation in the problem at face value. Don't read too much into it. These problems will not require you to make huge leaps of logic. The test writers aren't trying to throw you off with a cheap trick. If you have to go beyond creativity and make a leap of logic in order to have an answer choice answer the question, then you should look at the other answer choices. Don't overcomplicate the problem by creating theoretical relationships or explanations that will warp time or space. These are normal problems rooted in reality. It's just that the applicable relationship or explanation may not be readily apparent and you have to figure things out. Use your common sense to interpret anything that isn't clear.

Prefixes

If you're having trouble with a word in the question or answer choices, try dissecting it. Take advantage of every clue that the word might include. Prefixes and suffixes can be a huge help. Usually they allow you to determine a basic meaning. Pre- means before, post- means after, pro - is positive, de- is negative. From these prefixes and suffixes, you can get an idea of the general meaning of the word and try to put it into context. Beware though of any traps. Just because con is the opposite of pro, doesn't necessarily mean congress is the opposite of progress!

Hedge Phrases

Watch out for critical "hedge" phrases, such as likely, may, can, will often, sometimes, often, almost, mostly, usually, generally, rarely, sometimes. Question writers insert these hedge phrases to cover every possibility. Often an answer choice will be wrong simply because it leaves no room for exception. Avoid answer choices that have definitive words like "exactly," and "always".

Switchback Words

Stay alert for "switchbacks". These are the words and phrases frequently used to alert you to shifts in thought. The most common switchback word is "but". Others include although, however, nevertheless, on the other hand, even though, while, in spite of, despite, regardless of.

New Information

Correct answer choices will rarely have completely new information included. Answer choices typically are straightforward reflections of the material asked about and will directly relate to the question. If a new piece of information is included in an answer choice that doesn't even seem to relate to the topic being asked about, then that answer choice is likely incorrect. All of the information needed to answer the question is usually provided for you, and so you should not have to make guesses that are unsupported or choose answer choices that require unknown information that cannot be reasoned on its own.

Time Management

On technical questions, don't get lost on the technical terms. Don't spend too much time on any one question. If you don't know what a term means, then since you don't have a dictionary, odds are you aren't going to get much further. You should immediately recognize terms as whether or not you know them. If you don't, work with the other clues that you have, the other answer choices and terms provided, but don't waste too much time trying to figure out a difficult term.

Contextual Clues

Look for contextual clues. An answer can be right but not correct. The contextual clues will help you find the answer that is most right and is correct. Understand the context in which a phrase or statement is made. This will help you make important distinctions.

Don't Panic

Panicking will not answer any questions for you. Therefore, it isn't helpful. When you first see the question, if your mind goes blank, take a deep breath. Force yourself to mechanically go through the steps of solving the problem and using the strategies you've learned.

Pace Yourself

Don't get clock fever. It's easy to be overwhelmed when you're looking at a page full of questions, your mind is full of random thoughts and feeling confused, and the clock is ticking down faster than you would like. Calm down and maintain the pace that you have set for yourself. As long as you are on track by monitoring your pace, you are guaranteed to have enough time for yourself. When you get to the last few minutes of the test, it may seem like you won't have enough time left, but if you only have as many questions as you should have left at that point, then you're right on track!

Answer Selection

The best way to pick an answer choice is to eliminate all of those that are wrong, until only one is left and confirm that is the correct answer. Sometimes though, an answer choice may immediately look right. Be careful! Take a second to make sure that the other choices are not equally obvious. Don't make a hasty mistake. There are only two times that you should stop before checking other answers. First is when you are positive that the answer choice you have selected is correct. Second is when time is almost out and you have to make a quick guess!

Check Your Work

Since you will probably not know every term listed and the answer to every question, it is important that you get credit for the ones that you do know. Don't miss any questions through careless mistakes. If at all possible, try to take a second to look back over your answer selection and make sure you've selected the correct answer choice and haven't made a costly careless mistake (such as marking an answer choice that you didn't mean to mark). This quick double check should more than pay for itself in caught mistakes for the time it costs.

Beware of Directly Quoted Answers

Sometimes an answer choice will repeat word for word a portion of the question or reference section. However, beware of such exact duplication – it may be a trap! More than likely, the correct choice will paraphrase or summarize a point, rather than being exactly the same wording.

Slang

Scientific sounding answers are better than slang ones. An answer choice that begins "To compare the outcomes…" is much more likely to be correct than one that begins "Because some people insisted…"

Extreme Statements

Avoid wild answers that throw out highly controversial ideas that are proclaimed as established fact. An answer choice that states the "process should be used in certain situations, if…" is much more likely to be correct than one that states the "process should be discontinued completely." The first is a calm rational statement and doesn't even make a definitive, uncompromising stance, using a hedge word "if" to provide wiggle room, whereas the second choice is a radical idea and far more extreme.

Answer Choice Families

When you have two or more answer choices that are direct opposites or parallels, one of them is usually the correct answer. For instance, if one answer choice states "x increases" and another answer choice states "x decreases" or "y increases," then those two or three answer choices are very similar in construction and fall into the same family of answer choices. A family of answer choices is when two or three answer choices are very similar in construction, and yet often have a directly opposite meaning. Usually the correct answer choice will be in that family of answer choices. The "odd man out" or answer choice that doesn't seem to fit the parallel construction of the other answer choices is more likely to be incorrect.

Special Report: What Your Test Score Will Tell You About Your IQ

Did you know that most standardized tests correlate very strongly with IQ? In fact, your general intelligence is a better predictor of your success than any other factor, and most tests intentionally measure this trait to some degree to ensure that those selected by the test are truly qualified for the test's purposes.

Before we can delve into the relation between your test score and IQ, I will first have to explain what exactly is IQ. Here's the formula:

Your IQ = 100 + (Number of standard deviations below or above the average)*15

Now, let's define standard deviations by using an example. If we have 5 people with 5 different heights, then first we calculate the average. Let's say the average was 65 inches. The standard deviation is the "average distance" away from the average of each of the members. It is a direct measure of variability - if the 5 people included Jackie Chan and Shaquille O'Neal, obviously there's a lot more variability in that group than a group of 5 sisters who are all within 6 inches in height of each other. The standard deviation uses a number to characterize the average range of difference within a group.

A convenient feature of most groups is that they have a "normal" distribution- makes sense that most things would be normal, right? Without getting into a bunch of statistical mumbo-jumbo, you just need to know that if you know the average of the group and the standard deviation, you can successfully predict someone's percentile rank in the group.

Confused? Let me give you an example. If instead of 5 people's heights, we had 100 people, we could figure out their rank in height JUST by knowing the average, standard deviation, and their height. We wouldn't need to know each person's height and manually rank them, we could just predict their rank based on three numbers.

What this means is that you can take your PERCENTILE rank that is often given with your test and relate this to your RELATIVE IQ of people taking the test - that is, your IQ relative to the people taking the test. Obviously, there's no way to know your actual IQ because the people taking a standardized test are usually not very good samples of the general population- many of those with extremely low IQ's never achieve a level of success or competency necessary to complete a typical standardized test. In fact, professional psychologists who measure IQ actually have to use non-written tests that can fairly measure the IQ of those not able to complete a traditional test.

The bottom line is to not take your test score too seriously, but it is fun to compute your "relative IQ" among the people who took the test with you. I've done the calculations below. Just look up your percentile rank in the left and then you'll see your "relative IQ" for your test in the right hand column-

Percentile Rank	Your Relative IQ		Percentile Rank	Your Relative IQ
99	135		59	103
98	131		58	103
97	128		57	103
96	126		56	102
95	125		55	102
94	123		54	102
93	122		53	101
92	121		52	101
91	120		51	100
90	119		50	100
89	118		49	100
88	118		48	99
87	117		47	99
86	116		46	98
85	116		45	98
84	115		44	98
83	114		43	97
82	114		42	97
81	113		41	97
80	113		40	96
79	112		39	96
78	112		38	95
77	111		37	95
76	111		36	95
75	110		35	94
74	110		34	94
73	109		33	93
72	109		32	93
71	108		31	93
70	108		30	92
69	107		29	92
68	107		28	91
67	107		27	91
66	106		26	90
65	106		25	90
64	105		24	89
63	105		23	89
62	105		22	88
61	104		21	88
60	104		20	87

Special Report: Retaking the Test: What Are Your Chances at Improving Your Score?

After going through the experience of taking a major test, many test takers feel that once is enough. The test usually comes during a period of transition in the test taker's life, and taking the test is only one of a series of important events. With so many distractions and conflicting recommendations, it may be difficult for a test taker to rationally determine whether or not he should retake the test after viewing his scores.

The importance of the test usually only adds to the burden of the retake decision. However, don't be swayed by emotion. There a few simple questions that you can ask yourself to guide you as you try to determine whether a retake would improve your score:

1. What went wrong? Why wasn't your score what you expected?

Can you point to a single factor or problem that you feel caused the low score? Were you sick on test day? Was there an emotional upheaval in your life that caused a distraction? Were you late for the test or not able to use the full time allotment? If you can point to any of these specific, individual problems, then a retake should definitely be considered.

2. Is there enough time to improve?

Many problems that may show up in your score report may take a lot of time for improvement. A deficiency in a particular math skill may require weeks or months of tutoring and studying to improve. If you have enough time to improve an identified weakness, then a retake should definitely be considered.

3. How will additional scores be used? Will a score average, highest score, or most recent score be used?

Different test scores may be handled completely differently. If you've taken the test multiple times, sometimes your highest score is used, sometimes your average score is computed and used, and sometimes your most recent score is used. Make sure you understand what method will be used to evaluate your scores, and use that to help you determine whether a retake should be considered.

4. Are my practice test scores significantly higher than my actual test score?

If you have taken a lot of practice tests and are consistently scoring at a much higher level than your actual test score, then you should consider a retake. However, if you've taken five practice tests and only one of your scores was higher than your actual test score, or if your practice test scores were only slightly higher than your actual test score, then it is unlikely that you will significantly increase your score.

5. Do I need perfect scores or will I be able to live with this score? Will this score still allow me to follow my dreams?

What kind of score is acceptable to you? Is your current score "good enough?" Do you have to have a certain score in order to pursue the future of your dreams? If you won't be happy with your current score, and there's no way that you could live with it, then you should consider a retake. However, don't get your hopes up. If you are looking for significant improvement, that may or may not be possible. But if you won't be happy otherwise, it is at least worth the effort.
Remember that there are other considerations. To achieve your dream, it is likely that your grades may also be taken into account. A great test score is usually not the only thing necessary to succeed. Make sure that you aren't overemphasizing the importance of a high test score.

Furthermore, a retake does not always result in a higher score. Some test takers will score lower on a retake, rather than higher. One study shows that one-fourth of test takers will achieve a significant improvement in test score, while one-sixth of test takers will actually show a decrease. While this shows that most test takers will improve, the majority will only improve their scores a little and a retake may not be worth the test taker's effort.

Finally, if a test is taken only once and is considered in the added context of good grades on the part of a test taker, the person reviewing the grades and scores may be tempted to assume that the test taker just had a bad day while taking the test, and may discount the low test score in favor of the high grades. But if the test is retaken and the scores are approximately the same, then the validity of the low scores are only confirmed. Therefore, a retake could actually hurt a test taker by definitely bracketing a test taker's score ability to a limited range.

Special Report: Ethics Research and Websites

Business Ethics Resources on WWW
Links to sites in the areas of codes of ethics, organizations, publications, specific topics, and papers.
http://www.ethics.ubc.ca/resources/business

Discussions of Ethics on the Net
List of Internet discussion groups with links and subscription addresses.
http://frank.mtsu.edu/~jpurcell/Ethics/ethics.html

Ethics Resources on the Net
Links to sites in areas of business ethics such as codes of conduct, reference sources, organizations, issues, corporations, consultants, and commentaries. Also includes links to other types of ethics sites
(human rights, environment, etc.)
http://www.depaul.edu/ethics/

Ethikos and Corporate Conduct Quarterly
http://www.singerpubs.com/ethikos

The On-Line Journal of Ethics
http://condor.depaul.edu/ethics/ethg1.html

The Newsletter of DePaul University's Institute for Business & Professional Ethics
http://www.depaul.edu/ethics/newslet.html

Organizations

Note: Each summary is taken from material on the organization's web site.

Caux Round Table
Senior business leaders from Europe, Japan, and North America who are committed to the promotion of principled business leadership.
http://www.cauxroundtable.org

DePaul University's Institute for Business and Professional Ethics
The mission of the Institute is to foster ethical behavior by providing for and participating

in ethics-related education, offering resources to stakeholders (e.g. conferences, lecture series, on-site training, discussion and written materials), and supporting and disseminating cutting-edge scholarship of ethical relevance.
http://www.depaul.edu/ethics

European Business Ethics Network
Its role is to stimulate and facilitate meetings of minds, discussion and debate on common ethical problems and dilemmas. Network members include business people, public sector managers, and academics.
http://www.nijenrode.nl/research/eibe/eben/index.html

International Business Ethics Institute
Its mission is to foster global business practices which promote equitable economic development, resource sustainability and democratic forms of government.
http://www.business-ethics.org

International Society of Business, Economics and Ethics
The aim of the Society is to facilitate the dissemination of information and to foster interaction among businesses, academics, professional societies, and others interested in the ethical dimensions of business and economics on the international level.
http://www.nd.edu/~isbee

Center for Ethical Business Cultures
Assists business leaders in developing practical, productive and responsible relationships with key stakeholders.
http://www.stthomas.edu/www/mccr_http/index.html

Transparency International
Acts to counter corruption, both in international business transactions and at national levels.
http://www.transparency.de

University of British Columbia's Centre for Applied Ethics
The mission of the Centre is to bring moral philosophy into the public domain by advancing research in applied ethics, supporting courses with a significant ethical component and acting as a community resource.
http://www.ethics.ubc.ca

University of St. Thomas Koch Endowed Chair
in Business Ethics
The Koch Endowed Chair in Business Ethics works with other entities on campus to ensure

that ethics education remains a priority through business ethics education in both the undergraduate and MBA programs, faculty development, and the promotion of responsible corporate citizenship through
professional development opportunities and other events.
http://www.gsb.stthomas.edu/ethics

Wharton Ethics Program
The Wharton School supports its commitment to the discussion of the ethical issues that confront business through its courses, faculty, research, and publications.
http://rider.wharton.upenn.edu/~ethics

Special Report: Executive Search and Websites

Atlantic Research Technologies (http://www.atlanticresearch.com)
Worldwide executive search and management recruitment in over 1,000 top world markets, for the high tech, industrial and service sector.

Busch International (http://www.buschint.com)
An executive search firm serving the Investment, High Technology & Venture community since 1985. Services dynamic companies that are experiencing rapid growth (or have that potential) and to companies that need key individuals to lead expansion and valuation.

Dunhill Professional Search of Houston, NW (http://www.dunhillhouston.com/)
As an executive search firm, we are different from your stereotypical "headhunter" or "employment agency". We only recruit the best candidates for each company's specific employment needs. Furthermore, we make sure the candidate's style and the company's culture are a perfect match.

Global Executive Services (http://www.globalexecserv.com)
GES is a vertical Technology, IT, including Sales & Marketing search & placement firm, across multiple industries with a focus on Fortune 100, consulting, startup and corporate companies.

IR2000 (http://www.IR2000.com)
IR2000 offers consulting services for Companies seeking exceptionally qualified candidates. Our focus is to supplement the client's recruitment efforts by creating an employee focused search effort.

King Executive Search, Inc. (http://www.king-search.com)
A retained executive search firm. Working in partnership with our clients allows us to help them identify, assess and hire the best possible candidates.

Orion Recruiting Group, The (http://www.orionrecruitinggroup.com)
A national contingency executive search and human capital consulting. We will handle everything from recruiting the candidate, scheduling interviews, and especially the successful placement and start day of the candidate.

Quest (http://www.QuestCareer.com)
Contingency-based executive recruiter search firm for sales, marketing, IT, and engineering positions in Minnesota. Specializes in candidates with 2 years or more years experience at

salaries of $50,000 and above.

Red Rock Management (http://www.redrockmanagement.biz)
Red Rock Managment brings candidates and clients together in the Healthcare, Managed Care, Actuary & Human Resources career fields. We work nationwide!

Spanusa (http://www.spanusa.net)
An executive search firm specializing in the placement of bilingual (Spanish/English and Portuguese/English) professionals working in all industries and functions.

Strategic Executive Search (http://www.sesasia.com/)
Leading Asia-based executive search practice with office throughout Greater China.

Talisman Retail (http://www.wholeofthemoon.co.uk)
London UK & International retail recruitment agency - fashion, design, buying, executive, management and textile jobs.

The Perkins Group (http://www.perkinsgroup.com/)
A nationally recognized firm specializing in the manufacturing industries. Being generalists, we focus in manufacturing, distribution/logistics, engineering, human resources, accounting/finance and information technology.

Trainor/Frank & Associates, Inc (http://www.trainorfrank.com)
Trainor/Frank provides executive search and HR consulting solutions on a national level.

Valerie Frederickson & Company (http://www.vfandco.com/)
Services include retained executive search, human resource consulting, human resource contracting, succession planning, management and leadership development, organizational development, executive coaching, career management consulting and outplacement.

Special Report: Key Formulas

COST FORMULAS	
CV = Cost Variance	**EV - AC**
A negative variance indicates a cost overrun	BCWP -ACWP
(+ under budget, - over budget)	
SV = Schedule Variance	**EV - PV**
(> 0 = ahead of schedule; < 0 behind schedule)	BCWP-BCWS
If CV is positive and SV is negative	Either the task has not started or it has started and not enough resources have been applied
If CV is negative and SV is negative	The costs are overrun and the schedule is slipping
If CV is negative and SV is positive	This indicates that money was spent to crash the schedule
If CV is positive and SV is positive	The project is under budget and ahead of schedule
CPI = Cost Performance Index	**EV/AC**
(=1.0 perfect performance, < 1.0 poor, > 1.0 exceptional)	BCWP/ACWP
How efficient is my cost	

SPI = Schedule Performance Index	**EV/PV**
(-1.0 perfect performance, <1.0 poor, > 1.0 exceptional)	BCWP/BCWS
How efficient is my schedule	
EAC = Estimate At Completion	**AC + ETC**
	This formula is used when past performance shows that the original estimating assumptions were fundamentally flawed or that they are no longer relevant because of a change in conditions; Actuals to date plus a new estimate for all remaining work.
	AC + (BAC - EV)/CPI (where CPI is cumulative CPI)
	This formula is used when current variances are seen as typical of future variances; Modified by a performance factor.
	AC + BAC - EV
	This formula is used when current variances are seen as atypical and Project Manager's team expectation is that similar variances will not occur in the future; Actuals to date plus remaining budget (BAC-EV)
ETC = Estimate to Complete	**BAC - EV**
	(BAC-BCWP) /CPI
BAC = Budget at Completion	Sum of total project budget
VAC = Variance At Completion	VAC = BAC - EAC
How far off will I be at the end of the project?	

CV% = Cost Variance Percentage	CV% = CV/EV*100
How far off is my cost?	
SV% = Schedule Variance Percentage	SV% = SV/PV*100
How far off is my schedule?	
VAC% = Variance At Completion Percentage	VAC% = VAC/BAC*100

Variable and Type	Earned Value Description
PV = Planned Value (BCWS)	The cost of what I planned to get done
EV = Earned Value (BCWP)	The value of the work actually done
AC = Actual Cost (ACWP)	The totals of costs incurred in a given period

Other Formulas	
Straight Line Depreciation	Cost- Salvage/Time
Double Declining Balance	Double the SL Depreciation; $ X original cost - accumulated depreciation
Sum of Years (SOY)	(Cost-Salvage) X year/sum of years (3-2-1/6)
Future Value	D(r+1) to the # of periods
Simple Interest	Interest = Principle X Rate X Time
Compound Interest	FV (Future Value) = Deposit (1 + rate) ; Principle/ (r+1) to the # of periods
Communication Channels	# Of Team Members (t) X (t-1)/2
Expected Value	Optimistic + (4XMost Likely) + Pessimistic/6
Standard Deviation	Optimistic-Pessimistic/6 (one deviation is the difference between EV and SD)

Standard Deviations	68.26, 95.46, 99.73
Variance	Planned - Actual; % Variance = Variance/Planned
EMV = Expected Monetary Value	probability X amount of Stake (probability is frequency/# of possible; amount at stake = cost of loss and least cost to restore
NPV = Net Present Value	Initial payment of 12,000, annual discount rate of 10-% cost or revenue/(1-r) to the t
	Sometimes called discounted cash flows, assumes that there is a minimum desired rate of return and that all future cash flows are discounted to the present time. It is the sum of all the discounted cash flows, both outgoing and incoming, over the life of the project.

Special Report: What is Test Anxiety and How to Overcome It?

The very nature of tests caters to some level of anxiety, nervousness or tension, just as we feel for any important event that occurs in our lives. A little bit of anxiety or nervousness can be a good thing. It helps us with motivation, and makes achievement just that much sweeter. However, too much anxiety can be a problem; especially if it hinders our ability to function and perform.

"Test anxiety," is the term that refers to the emotional reactions that some test-takers experience when faced with a test or exam. Having a fear of testing and exams is based upon a rational fear, since the test-taker's performance can shape the course of an academic career. Nevertheless, experiencing excessive fear of examinations will only interfere with the test-takers ability to perform, and his/her chances to be successful.

There are a large variety of causes that can contribute to the development and sensation of test anxiety. These include, but are not limited to lack of performance and worrying about issues surrounding the test.

Lack of Preparation

Lack of preparation can be identified by the following behaviors or situations:

Not scheduling enough time to study, and therefore cramming the night before the test or exam
Managing time poorly, to create the sensation that there is not enough time to do everything
Failing to organize the text information in advance, so that the study material consists of the entire text and not simply the pertinent information
Poor overall studying habits

Worrying, on the other hand, can be related to both the test taker, or many other factors around him/her that will be affected by the results of the test. These include worrying about:

There are three primary elements to test anxiety. Physical components, which involve the same typical bodily reactions as those to acute anxiety (to be discussed below).

Emotional factors have to do with fear or panic. Mental or cognitive issues concerning attention spans and memory abilities.

Physical Signals

There are many different symptoms of test anxiety, and these are not limited to mental and emotional strain. Frequently there are a range of physical signals that will let a test taker know that he/she is suffering from test anxiety. These bodily changes can include the following:

Perspiring
Sweaty palms
Wet, trembling hands
Nausea
Dry mouth
A knot in the stomach
Headache
Faintness
Muscle tension
Aching shoulders, back and neck
Rapid heart beat
Feeling too hot/cold

To recognize the sensation of test anxiety, a test-taker should monitor him/herself for the following sensations:

The physical distress symptoms as listed above
Emotional sensitivity, expressing emotional feelings such as the need to cry or laugh too much, or a sensation of anger or helplessness
A decreased ability to think, causing the test-taker to blank out or have racing thoughts that are hard to organize or control.

Though most students will feel some level of anxiety when faced with a test or exam, the majority can cope with that anxiety and maintain it at a manageable level. However, those who cannot are faced with a very real and very serious condition, which can and should be controlled for the immeasurable benefit of this sufferer.

Naturally, these sensations lead to negative results for the testing experience. The most common effects of test anxiety have to do with nervousness and mental blocking.

Nervousness

Nervousness can appear in several different levels:

The test-taker's difficulty, or even inability to read and understand the questions on the test
The difficulty or inability to organize thoughts to a coherent form
The difficulty or inability to recall key words and concepts relating to the testing questions (especially essays)
The receipt of poor grades on a test, though the test material was well known by the test taker

Conversely, a person may also experience mental blocking, which involves:

Blanking out on test questions
Only remembering the correct answers to the questions when the test has already finished.

Fortunately for test anxiety sufferers, beating these feelings, to a large degree, has to do with proper preparation. When a test taker has a feeling of preparedness, then anxiety will be dramatically lessened.

The first step to resolving anxiety issues is to distinguish which of the two types of anxiety are being suffered. If the anxiety is a direct result of a lack of preparation, this should be considered a normal reaction, and the anxiety level (as opposed to the test results) shouldn't be anything to worry about. However, if, when adequately prepared, the test-taker still panics, blanks out, or seems to overreact, this is not a fully rational reaction. While this can be considered normal too, there are many ways to combat and overcome these effects.

Remember that anxiety cannot be entirely eliminated, however, there are ways to minimize it, to make the anxiety easier to manage. Preparation is one of the best ways to minimize test anxiety. Therefore the following techniques are wise in order to best fight off any anxiety that may want to build.

To begin with, try to avoid cramming before a test, whenever it is possible. By trying to memorize an entire term's worth of information in one day, you'll be shocking your system, and not giving yourself a very good chance to absorb the information. This is an easy path to anxiety, so for those who suffer from test anxiety, cramming should not even be considered an option.

Instead of cramming, work throughout the semester to combine all of the material which is presented throughout the semester, and work on it gradually as the course goes by, making sure to master the main concepts first, leaving minor details for a week or so before the test.

To study for the upcoming exam, be sure to pose questions that may be on the examination, to gauge the ability to answer them by integrating the ideas from your texts, notes and lectures, as well as any supplementary readings.

If it is truly impossible to cover all of the information that was covered in that particular term, concentrate on the most important portions, that can be covered very well. Learn these concepts as best as possible, so that when the test comes, a goal can be made to use these concepts as presentations of your knowledge.

In addition to study habits, changes in attitude are critical to beating a struggle with test anxiety. In fact, an improvement of the perspective over the entire test-taking experience can actually help a test taker to enjoy studying and therefore improve the overall experience. Be certain not to overemphasize the significance of the grade - know that the result of the test is neither a reflection of self worth, nor is it a measure of intelligence; one grade will not predict a person's future success.

To improve an overall testing outlook, the following steps should be tried:

Keeping in mind that the most reasonable expectation for taking a test is to expect to try to demonstrate as much of what you know as you possibly can.
Reminding ourselves that a test is only one test; this is not the only one, and there will be others.
The thought of thinking of oneself in an irrational, all-or-nothing term should be avoided at all costs.
A reward should be designated for after the test, so there's something to look forward to. Whether it be going to a movie, going out to eat, or simply visiting friends, schedule it in advance, and do it no matter what result is expected on the exam.

Test-takers should also keep in mind that the basics are some of the most important things, even beyond anti-anxiety techniques and studying. Never neglect the basic social, emotional and biological needs, in order to try to absorb information. In order to best achieve, these three factors must be held as just as important as the studying itself.

Study Steps

Remember the following important steps for studying:

Maintain healthy nutrition and exercise habits. Continue both your recreational activities and social pass times. These both contribute to your physical and emotional well being.

Be certain to get a good amount of sleep, especially the night before the test, because when you're overtired you are not able to perform to the best of your best ability.

Keep the studying pace to a moderate level by taking breaks when they are needed, and varying the work whenever possible, to keep the mind fresh instead of getting bored. When enough studying has been done that all the material that can be learned has been learned, and the test taker is prepared for the test, stop studying and do something relaxing such as listening to music, watching a movie, or taking a warm bubble bath.

There are also many other techniques to minimize the uneasiness or apprehension that is experienced along with test anxiety before, during, or even after the examination. In fact, there are a great deal of things that can be done to stop anxiety from interfering with lifestyle and performance. Again, remember that anxiety will not be eliminated entirely, and it shouldn't be. Otherwise that "up" feeling for exams would not exist, and most of us depend on that sensation to perform better than usual. However, this anxiety has to be at a level that is manageable.

Of course, as we have just discussed, being prepared for the exam is half the battle right away. Attending all classes, finding out what knowledge will be expected on the exam, and knowing the exam schedules are easy steps to lowering anxiety. Keeping up with work will remove the need to cram, and efficient study habits will eliminate wasted time. Studying should be done in an ideal location for concentration, so that it is simple to become interested in the material and give it complete attention. A method such as SQ3R (Survey, Question, Read, Recite, Review) is a wonderful key to follow to make sure that the study habits are as effective as possible, especially in the case of learning from a textbook. Flashcards are great techniques for memorization. Learning to take good notes will mean that notes will be full of useful information, so that less sifting will need to be done to seek out what is pertinent for studying. Reviewing notes after class and then again on occasion will keep the information fresh in the mind. From notes that have been taken summary sheets and outlines can be made for simpler reviewing.

A study group can also be a very motivational and helpful place to study, as there will be a sharing of ideas, all of the minds can work together, to make sure that everyone understands, and the studying will be made more interesting because it will be a social occasion.

Basically, though, as long as the test-taker remains organized and self confident, with efficient study habits, less time will need to be spent studying, and higher grades will be achieved.

To become self confident, there are many useful steps. The first of these is "self talk." It has been shown through extensive research, that self-talk for students who suffer from test anxiety, should be well monitored, in order to make sure that it contributes to self confidence as opposed to sinking the student. Frequently the self talk of test-anxious students is negative or self-defeating, thinking that everyone else is smarter and faster, that they always mess up, and that if they don't do well, they'll fail the entire course. It is important to decreasing anxiety that awareness is made of self talk. Try writing any negative self thoughts and then disputing them with a positive statement instead. Begin self-encouragement as though it was a friend speaking. Repeat positive statements to help reprogram the mind to believing in successes instead of failures.

Helpful Techniques

Other extremely helpful techniques include:

Self-visualization of doing well and reaching goals
While aiming for an "A" level of understanding, don't try to "overprotect" by setting your expectations lower. This will only convince the mind to stop studying in order to meet the lower expectations.
Don't make comparisons with the results or habits of other students. These are individual factors, and different things work for different people, causing different results.
Strive to become an expert in learning what works well, and what can be done in order to improve. Consider collecting this data in a journal.
Create rewards for after studying instead of doing things before studying that will only turn into avoidance behaviors.
Make a practice of relaxing - by using methods such as progressive relaxation, self-hypnosis, guided imagery, etc - in order to make relaxation an automatic sensation.
Work on creating a state of relaxed concentration so that concentrating will take on the focus of the mind, so that none will be wasted on worrying.
Take good care of the physical self by eating well and getting enough sleep.
Plan in time for exercise and stick to this plan.

Beyond these techniques, there are other methods to be used before, during and after the test that will help the test-taker perform well in addition to overcoming anxiety.

Before the exam comes the academic preparation. This involves establishing a study schedule and beginning at least one week before the actual date of the test. By doing this, the anxiety of not having enough time to study for the test will be automatically eliminated. Moreover, this will make the studying a much more effective experience, ensuring that the learning will be an easier process. This relieves much undue pressure on the test-taker.

Summary sheets, note cards, and flash cards with the main concepts and examples of these main concepts should be prepared in advance of the actual studying time. A topic should never be eliminated from this process. By omitting a topic because it isn't expected to be on the test is only setting up the test-taker for anxiety should it actually appear on the exam. Utilize the course syllabus for laying out the topics that should be studied. Carefully go over the notes that were made in class, paying special attention to any of the issues that the professor took special care to emphasize while lecturing in class. In the textbooks, use the chapter review, or if possible, the chapter tests, to begin your review.

It may even be possible to ask the instructor what information will be covered on the exam, or what the format of the exam will be (for example, multiple choice, essay, free form, true-false). Additionally, see if it is possible to find out how many questions will be on the test. If a review sheet or sample test has been offered by the professor, make good use of it, above anything else, for the preparation for the test. Another great resource for getting to know the examination is reviewing tests from previous semesters. Use these tests to review, and aim to achieve a 100% score on each of the possible topics. With a few exceptions, the goal that you set for yourself is the highest one that you will reach.

Take all of the questions that were assigned as homework, and rework them to any other possible course material. The more problems reworked, the more skill and confidence will form as a result. When forming the solution to a problem, write out each of the steps. Don't simply do head work. By doing as many steps on paper as possible, much clarification and therefore confidence will be formed. Do this with as many homework problems as possible, before checking the answers. By checking the answer after each problem, a reinforcement will exist, that will not be on the exam. Study situations should be as exam-like as possible, to prime the test-taker's system for the experience. By waiting to check the answers at the end, a psychological advantage will be formed, to decrease the stress factor.

Another fantastic reason for not cramming is the avoidance of confusion in concepts, especially when it comes to mathematics. 8-10 hours of study will become one hundred percent more effective if it is spread out over a week or at least several days, instead of doing it all in one sitting. Recognize that the human brain requires time in order to assimilate new material, so frequent breaks and a span of study time over several days will be much more beneficial.

Additionally, don't study right up until the point of the exam. Studying should stop a minimum of one hour before the exam begins. This allows the brain to rest and put things in their proper order. This will also provide the time to become as relaxed as possible when going into the examination room. The test-taker will also have time to eat well and eat sensibly. Know that the brain needs food as much as the rest of the body. With enough food and enough sleep, as well as a relaxed attitude, the body and the mind are primed for success.

Avoid any anxious classmates who are talking about the exam. These students only spread anxiety, and are not worth sharing the anxious sentimentalities.

Before the test also involves creating a positive attitude, so mental preparation should also be a point of concentration. There are many keys to creating a positive attitude. Should fears become rushing in, make a visualization of taking the exam, doing well, and seeing an A written on the paper. Write out a list of affirmations that will bring a feeling of confidence, such as "I am doing well in my English class," "I studied well and know my material," "I enjoy this class." Even if the affirmations aren't believed at first, it sends a positive message to the subconscious which will result in an alteration of the overall belief system, which is the system that creates reality.

If a sensation of panic begins, work with the fear and imagine the very worst! Work through the entire scenario of not passing the test, failing the entire course, and dropping out of school, followed by not getting a job, and pushing a shopping cart through the dark alley where you'll live. This will place things into perspective! Then, practice deep breathing and create a visualization of the opposite situation - achieving an "A" on the exam, passing the entire course, receiving the degree at a graduation ceremony.

On the day of the test, there are many things to be done to ensure the best results, as well as the most calm outlook. The following stages are suggested in order to maximize test-taking potential:

Begin the examination day with a moderate breakfast, and avoid any coffee or beverages with caffeine if the test taker is prone to jitters. Even people who are used to managing caffeine can feel jittery or light-headed when it is taken on a test day. Attempt to do something that is relaxing before the examination begins. As last minute cramming clouds the mastering of overall concepts, it is better to use this time to create a calming outlook.

Be certain to arrive at the test location well in advance, in order to provide time to select a location that is away from doors, windows and other distractions, as well as giving enough time to relax before the test begins.

Keep away from anxiety generating classmates who will upset the sensation of stability and relaxation that is being attempted before the exam.

Should the waiting period before the exam begins cause anxiety, create a self-distraction by reading a light magazine or something else that is relaxing and simple.

During the exam itself, read the entire exam from beginning to end, and find out how much time should be allotted to each individual problem. Once writing the exam, should more time be taken for a problem, it should be abandoned, in order to begin another problem. If there is time at the end, the unfinished problem can always be returned to and completed.

Read the instructions very carefully - twice - so that unpleasant surprises won't follow during or after the exam has ended.

When writing the exam, pretend that the situation is actually simply the completion of homework within a library, or at home. This will assist in forming a relaxed atmosphere, and will allow the brain extra focus for the complex thinking function.

Begin the exam with all of the questions with which the most confidence is felt. This will build the confidence level regarding the entire exam and will begin a quality momentum. This will also create encouragement for trying the problems where uncertainty resides.

Going with the "gut instinct" is always the way to go when solving a problem. Second guessing should be avoided at all costs. Have confidence in the ability to do well.

For essay questions, create an outline in advance that will keep the mind organized and make certain that all of the points are remembered. For multiple choice, read every answer, even if the correct one has been spotted - a better one may exist.

Continue at a pace that is reasonable and not rushed, in order to be able to work carefully. Provide enough time to go over the answers at the end, to check for small errors that can be corrected.

Should a feeling of panic begin, breathe deeply, and think of the feeling of the body releasing sand through its pores. Visualize a calm, peaceful place, and include all of the sights, sounds and sensations of this image. Continue the deep breathing, and take a few minutes to continue this with closed eyes. When all is well again, return to the test.

If a "blanking" occurs for a certain question, skip it and move on to the next question. There will be time to return to the other question later. Get everything done that can be done, first, to guarantee all the grades that can be compiled, and to build all of the confidence possible. Then return to the weaker questions to build the marks from there.

Remember, one's own reality can be created, so as long as the belief is there, success will follow. And remember: anxiety can happen later, right now, there's an exam to be written!

After the examination is complete, whether there is a feeling for a good grade or a bad grade, don't dwell on the exam, and be certain to follow through on the reward that was promised...and enjoy it! Don't dwell on any mistakes that have been made, as there is nothing that can be done at this point anyway.

Additionally, don't begin to study for the next test right away. Do something relaxing for a while, and let the mind relax and prepare itself to begin absorbing information again.

From the results of the exam - both the grade and the entire experience, be certain to learn from what has gone on. Perfect studying habits and work some more on confidence in order to make the next examination experience even better than the last one.

Learn to avoid places where openings occurred for laziness, procrastination and day dreaming.

Use the time between this exam and the next one to better learn to relax, even learning to relax on cue, so that any anxiety can be controlled during the next exam. Learn how to relax the body. Slouch in your chair if that helps. Tighten and then relax all of the different muscle groups, one group at a time, beginning with the feet and then working all the way up to the neck and face. This will ultimately relax the muscles more than they were to begin with. Learn how to breathe deeply and comfortably, and focus on this breathing going in and out as a relaxing thought. With every exhale, repeat the word "relax."

As common as test anxiety is, it is very possible to overcome it. Make yourself one of the test-takers who overcome this frustrating hindrance.

Special Report: Additional Bonus Material

Due to our efforts to try to keep this book to a manageable length, we've created a link that will give you access to all of your additional bonus material.

Please visit http://www.mometrix.com/bonus948/pmp to access the information.